HOW TO WRITE AN
ESSAY

Also included in the Ultimate Style writing series:

ultimate style

HOW TO WRITE AN
ESSAY

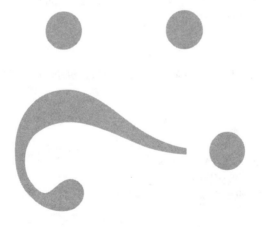

SPARK PUBLISHING

Written by Justin Marshall.
Parts of Chapter 8, Chapter 9, and Chapter 10 were written by
Tamar Schreibman and Doug Tarnopol.

Spark Publishing
A Division of Barnes & Noble Publishing
120 Fifth Avenue
New York, NY 10011
www.sparknotes.com

Please submit all comments and questions or report errors to
www.sparknotes.com/errors.

A full list of permission credits is on page 223.

Library of Congress Catalog-in-Publication Data

Marshall, Justin.
    Sparknotes ultimate style: how to write an essay / by Justin
    Marshall.
        p.cm.
    ISBN-13: 978-1-4114-9976-8
    ISBN-10: 1-4114-9976-X
 1. English language-Rhetoric. 2. Essay—Authorship.
 3. Report writing
 I. Title: How to write an essay. II. Title.

PE1471.M28 2006
808'.042—dc22

                                                        2005030714

Printed and bound in Canada.

  3 5 7 9 10 8 6 4 2

Acknowledgments

I didn't have the benefit of SparkNotes when I was learning to write essays, but I was blessed with many great teachers, among them Linda Ticer, Lindsay Russell, Douglas and Beverly Capelin, Robert Warde, and Annette Insdorf. Without their encouragement and tireless dedication, I never could have written this book. I am likewise very grateful to my colleagues and fellow teachers for their assistance and wisdom over the years, most notably Takeshi Nomoto, Andrea Moore Paldy, and Stephen Pite.

I owe sincere gratitude to all the people at SparkNotes, especially my editor, Margo Orlando. Her leadership and guidance were essential to this book, as were her generous contributions.

Lastly, I'd like to thank Mary Haas and my mother, Susan Marshall, for their unending love and support, as well as their honest critiques of my work over the years.

A Note from SparkNotes

F. Scott Fitzgerald once said, "All good writing is swimming under water and holding your breath." Maybe this is how you feel when you face a blank computer screen: desperate, a bit scared, and unable to breathe. Not to worry. Even world-famous essayists, researchers, fiction writers, and poets often feel this way. Writing isn't easy, and it takes a lot of work to write well. The good news is that writing is a skill you can learn.

That's where *SparkNotes Ultimate Style* comes in. We give you everything you need to know about how to write well, from thinking to planning to writing to revising. More important, we give it to you straight, in a concise, stripped-down style that tells you exactly what to do at every stage of the writing process. You won't find any ethereal, "writerly" advice in this book. Instead of "inspiration," we give you all the steps of the writing process, in the smarter, better, faster style you've come to rely on from SparkNotes.

SparkNotes Ultimate Style: How to Write an Essay is your key to writing great expository prose. We hope it gives you the confidence to write not only your first words but also your second and third and fourth … Your input makes us better. Let us know what you think at **www.sparknotes.com/comments**.

Contents

9 The College Admissions Essay 171

10 Crash Course in Grammar 207

A Final Note 221

Permission Credits 223

About the Author 225

Understanding the Essay

So: you have to write an essay. You're facing a blank computer screen and wracking your brain for a brilliant first sentence. Not so happy? You're not alone. Many students dread essay assignments, for two main reasons: essays require good writing, which takes work and practice, and, more important, they require critical *thinking*, sometimes about classes and subjects you know very little about. Instead of reviewing predetermined materials for an exam, you're left to your own devices to think more deeply about a subject and come up with an argument.

Relax: essay writing is a skill you can learn. No matter what kind of essay you're assigned to write, and no matter what you decide to write about, you first need to understand exactly what an essay *is*. You also need to know why essays are important, how essays are graded, and how great essays are structured. Once you know the basics, you'll be prepared to start writing an essay of your own.

Define the Essay

Essays take many forms, are printed in diverse places, and have numerous applications and purposes. Take a look at the *Merriam-Webster's Collegiate Dictionary* definition of *essay*:

ESSAY es • say *n*

an analytic or interpretative literary composition usually dealing with its subject from a limited or personal point of view

This definition leaves lots of room for ambiguity and confusion. To best understand what an essay *is*, you need to understand what it's *not*.

- An essay is *not* poetry or fiction. You figured that much out already.

Ultimate Style

- An essay is *not* a research paper. The primary purpose of a research paper is—you guessed it—research. While it incorporates the analytical, academic prose of an essay, its main objective is to evaluate how well you research and comprehend a topic. Sources and documentation are king.

- An essay is *not* a book report. Book reports are like research papers, but the research is based on a book, which you have to read and then summarize. While some "interpretive" prose is acceptable, the main goal is to document the plot, characters, and themes of the book. In the real world, these become reviews (of books, movies, plays, art, and other cultural events) that often appear in newspapers and magazines.

- An essay is *not* straightforward journalism. Most journalism endeavors to report facts without bias, interpretation, or a "point of view"—the antithesis of an essay. While essays are frequently found in journalistic publications, they tend to reside in specific pages (such as editorials) that are devoted to opinion.

Learn the Types

Essays come in all shapes and sizes, and you'll see them in nearly every publication you pick up. There are six basic types of essays:

1. Academic essays (including the SAT essay)
2. College admissions essays
3. Personal essays
4. Journalistic essays
5. Existential treatises
6. Letters to the editor

Each type of essay has its own unique characteristics and purposes, but all of them present a thesis and arguments to defend it.

Academic Essays   As a student, you're probably most familiar with this type of essay. The assignment is to argue and support a thesis on a given topic. Unlike a research paper, the emphasis is on *your own perspective*, not information gleaned from others. Depending on the assignment, these essays run from the very personal to the dry and academic. And an essay section has just been added to the SAT and ACT.

College Admissions Essays   We've included this as a separate category because the college admissions essay is a unique beast. While academic essays require you to illuminate an argument clearly and persuasively, college admissions essays require you to illuminate *you*. Far from being just a dry recounting of awards, accomplishments, and goals, this type of essay is most successful when you show some creativity and spark. A great college admissions essay is as individual as you are, but there are guidelines you can follow to maximize your chances of writing a stellar one.

Personal Essays   David Sedaris, Bill Bryson, and Dave Barry are all well known for their hilarious, offbeat essays on life as they see it around them. Comedians, novelists, and cultural icons as diverse as Jon Stewart, Mark Twain, and Garrison Keillor have all published essays as well, ranging from the political and cutting to the nostalgic and thoughtful. These types of essays tend to be more structurally free and observational than journalistic essays, and they appear in a wide range of publications, such as *The New Yorker*, the op-ed pages of newspapers, and even *Playboy*.

Ultimate Style

Personal Essay in Action   Essays come in many shapes and sizes and can cover any topic under the sun. This flexibility is the beauty of essays. Here's the first paragraph from "The Crack-Up," a personal essay by F. Scott Fitzgerald that discusses his mental breakdown:

> Of course all life is a process of breaking down, but the blows that do the dramatic side of the work—the big sudden blows that come, or seem to come, from outside—the ones you remember and blame things on and, in moments of weakness, tell your friends about, don't show their effect all at once. There

is another sort of blow that comes from within—that you don't feel until it's too late to do anything about it, until you realize with finality that in some regard you will never be as good a man again. The first sort of breakage seems to happen quick—the second kind happens without your knowing it but is realized suddenly indeed.

This is a personal essay, but Fitzgerald still sets it up with an intriguing introduction and a thesis. We understand that he's going to explain the nature of "breakages," as he calls them, and since the title is particular—"*The* Crack-Up" rather than "A Crack-Up"—we suspect he's going to explain his own experience with unhappiness. This is a solid essay beginning that ropes us in and sets us up for what we're about to read.

Journalistic Essays The journalistic essay is the opinionated cousin of straightforward investigative journalism. *Harper's* is an example of a magazine that publishes essays with a political bent; other publications focus on topics as diverse as film theory, religion, medicine, and science fiction. Journalistic essays are analytical and have a clear point of view.

Existential Treatises Existential treatises deal with more than just existentialism—they cover any serious subject that is contemplated and theorized upon in a more analytical than personal manner. James Baldwin and Richard Wright were known just as much for their essays on race as their fictional tales; Susan Sontag and Camille Paglia have considered feminism and gender studies; and Albert Camus and Immanuel

Kant dealt with philosophy. Some of the most famous historical essays fall into this category, including Henry David Thoreau's *Civil Disobedience* and Ralph Waldo Emerson's *Self-Reliance*.

Letters to the Editor   Although in letter form (they often begin with "Dear Editor"), these are essentially essays that provide readers' opinions on current issues. They have a clear point of view, and, if written well, are analytical. In this same category is the editorial, which is nothing more than a professional letter to the editor, written by a member of a periodical's staff.

Ultimate Style

Love the Essay

Unlike many of the skills you develop as a student (solving a trigonometric equation, for example), writing an essay has countless applications in the real world. Master the essay, and you'll feel qualified to take on any number of tasks—such as writing a letter to the editor of your local newspaper that will actually get published, or writing your memoirs for a magazine.

In short, *essays empower the student.* If you can master the structure, logic, and writing skills required to write a great essay, your chances of getting good grades and succeeding in many other subject areas are dramatically improved, whether you're good at a particular subject or not. And because essays become more prevalent at each higher level of education, even in math and the sciences, the skills you develop now will be even more valuable as your studies advance.

Understand the Grading

Essays are graded according to three basic criteria. Here they are, in order of importance:

1. Does the essay have a persuasive, convincing argument?
2. Does the essay showcase analytical thought?
3. Is the essay written well?

You'll notice that the list doesn't mention "showing you understand what you learned in class." This may come as a surprise, since in some ways an essay does reveal whether you've been paying attention in class. But the truth is different. If you write an essay with a persuasive argument using strong analytical skills, your instructor won't be able to deny the thesis—even if you never set foot in class. Similarly, if your essay touches on every concept covered in class but with flawed reasoning and a pathetic argument, it will suggest that you've learned nothing—even if you were in class every day. Knowing how to develop a *convincing, analytical argument* will make all the difference to your grade.

Deconstruct the Essay

All essays, no matter the type or topic, are pretty much identical in terms of construction. Master the construction, and you're halfway there. Toward this goal, it's time to introduce Dealin' Dan, your local used car salesman. You don't know him personally, but you've seen his TV commercials all too often. They're cheap, they come on only after 10:00 p.m., and they feature Dealin' Dan in an outdated suit, talking animatedly about his deals:

> *This is Dealin' Dan again, here to tell you that you can't afford to miss out on my year-end closeout! All our 2005 cars must go now, so I'm practically giving them away! Take fifteen percent off our already low prices! Five hundred dollars cash back! And if you don't see a deal you like, you make an offer—we won't refuse it! But stop by soon, 'cause with these Dealin' Dan deals, my cars won't be around for long!*

Ultimate Style

These commercials are bad—but they work. The key to Dan's success is that, whether he knows it or not, he has mastered the essay. He understands and carefully adheres to its basic, proven structure:

- A simple and coherent thesis statement
- Examples and reasoning to support the thesis statement
- A conclusion that summarizes all of this information

The Structure in Detail   At its core, essay structure is so simple that even Dealin' Dan can do it. Let's break down his commercial so we can see how closely he follows the rules.

> *This is Dealin' Dan again, here to tell you that you can't afford to miss out on my year-end closeout!*

This is Dan's thesis statement (his stance). He's simply inform-
ing us, his potential customers, as to why he's on TV: he's got a
great deal on cars. But we might be skeptical, so Dan can't just
tell us this and hope we believe it. He has to support his claim
with evidence:

> *All our 2005 cars must go now, so I'm practically giving them
> away! Take fifteen percent off our already low prices! Five
> hundred dollars cash back! And if you don't see a deal you like,
> you make an offer—we won't refuse it!*

Here, Dan supports his thesis with reasoning and examples. In
this particular ad, he begins with reasoning—explaining that
he *has to* sell last year's cars *now*. This isn't proof that his deals
are good, but we can logically deduce that if he has to sell the
cars fast, he's going to make compromises in the price. The
next three sentences contain specific examples: 15 percent off,
$500 cash back, and a promise that no offer will be refused.
Each of these points supports his initial statement that we can't
afford to miss his sale.

> *But stop by soon, 'cause with these Dealin' Dan deals, my cars
> won't be around for long!*

This is Dan's conclusion, and it's impressive. He doesn't restate
his thesis, nor does he try to sneak in another example. He
combines everything he's said thus far to form a new thought,
one that logically follows his reasoning: because his deals are
so good, we better go there ASAP. The best conclusions don't

merely summarize what has been said; they also hint at a new direction, potential future outcome, or unique perspective on the topic.

In a Nutshell   We'll explain the concepts of thesis, reasoning, and examples later in the book. For now, take a look at this chart to see what the structure of an essay *looks* like. An essay is divided into three main parts:

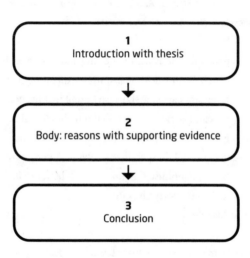

1
Introduction with thesis

2
Body: reasons with supporting evidence

3
Conclusion

Topics and Brainstorming

The topic is the heart of the essay—it determines the thesis, tone, and individual arguments. In other words, it determines practically *everything*. Whether you're given a topic to address or have to select one yourself, you need to think carefully about what the topic means to you. Creating an effective essay involves much more than writing a few paragraphs about the first idea that comes to your mind. Your topic can make or break your essay—so you need to consider it carefully.

Most essays are doomed before they're even written because the student has approached a given topic from a poorly thought-out direction or has chosen a topic that's too broad, too mundane, too banal, or just plain too bad. Understanding how to approach, choose, and narrow down your essay topic is vital to the essay-writing process—and will put you on the right path toward essay success.

Define the Assignment

Sometimes your instructor will select an essay topic for you, while other times, you'll have to choose one for yourself. Essay assignment topics generally fall into one of these three categories:

1. The open-ended topic: you decide.
2. The choose-one-of-three topic: you're provided with a few potential topics, and you choose one.
3. The predetermined topic: you have to write on exactly what you're told.

The main thing that differentiates these three categories is the level of control you have over the *choice* of topic, not the passion and enthusiasm you must have for it. Whether your topic comes from your own imagination or is forced upon you, you'll still have to find a way to connect to it. You have to figure out how to make that topic interesting—how to make that topic *your own*. If you don't, you'll be uninspired throughout the writing process, and your finished essay will be dull and lifeless.

Ultimate Style

Make Connections

When you make connections, you're creating a link between the material in class and your own interests in order to find a topic you'll be excited to write about. If you're taking a class you like, half of this process is done: your enjoyment of the subject almost guarantees you'll be able to find a topic that interests you. When it comes to subjects you can't stand, you have an extra challenge in finding an engaging topic. Either way, finding a topic that connects to or spurs your interests is an important step in writing an essay. When you're taking an exam, you just have to get the answers right to get a good grade. When you're writing an essay, however, you need to show some verve and energy. A lack of interest in the topic will show in every word you write.

Naturally, the less control you have over the choice of your topic, the harder it will be to make connections. But it can still be done. For example, if you have to write a paper on your least favorite philosopher, Descartes, go over his basic ideas and apply them to contemporary issues you're interested in—the environment, capital punishment, abortion. You're bound to find some link that you can exploit for the purposes of your essay.

Sparking Your Passions   One way to make connections and find a good topic is to find a parallel between the concepts of the class and your own passions. Let's say you're taking Introduction to Philosophy and your assignment is this:

> Choose one philosopher we studied in class and provide your thoughts on his or her most notable theories.

Easy enough—except that you hated every philosopher covered in class. To make connections, go over your notes and try to find a spark that catches your attention. You might find that while Aristotle and Descartes left you cold, there was an interesting tidbit in John Stuart Mill's *On Liberty*, where he suggested that governments must respect and preserve diversity at all costs. You feel strongly about the importance of diversity—especially in America's colleges and universities. If you create your thesis around this idea, you might be able to stay engaged, and connecting philosophy to an interest of your own will keep you interested enough to write an essay that's more thoughtful.

Create a Chart

Making connections between your interests and what you're studying is part of the brainstorming process. When you brainstorm, you let yourself "free think," coming up with lots of ideas for your essay. Your goal should be to come up with as many ideas as possible—don't reflect or censor yourself. You can figure out what ideas are actually possible when you narrow down your options. When you brainstorm, write everything down on a sheet of paper that you can keep with you through-out the writing process—this is your brainstorming chart.

While a brainstorming chart might seem to apply only to open-ended essays, it's actually a useful tool for all three kinds of essays. If you've been assigned a choose-one-of-three topic, a brainstorming chart will help you choose the topic that best connects to your interests and knowledge. You can brainstorm related subject areas and make connections to things you've done, read, seen, or been involved with. If you have *no* choice of topic, you'll see that a brainstorming chart will help you to come up with thoughts that will later form your thesis, reasons and examples, and arguments. You won't be brainstorming *topics*; you'll be brainstorming *ideas*. You can write down your initial impressions, along with the ideas those first impressions spur.

Finding Ideas   If you find you have only a handful of poten-tial topics and ideas, don't worry. Depending on the nature of the class and the specific assignment, you may be able to come up with only a few. To find more possibilities, consider these suggestions:

- Go over your class notes to find topics that may have been mentioned in discussions.
- Look at magazines and newspapers for ideas that spark your interest.
- Do some research online: look at newspapers from around the world, investigate websites related to your course, or find message boards to see what people are discussing.
- Talk to your friends and family. Even if they're not taking the same classes you are, they'll likely have some interesting ideas on the subject you're studying.

Brainstorming in Action   Your brainstorming chart will look different depending on what kind of assignment you're dealing with. Take a look at these examples:

Open-Ended Topic   *Write a five-page essay on an issue you feel strongly about.*

For this type of assignment, we simply list all the possible topics we can think of, without paying attention to whether or not they'd actually make good essays. Our goal is to get down as many ideas for topics as possible.

Potential Topics for Essay

World peace

Raising the minimum wage

The use of steroids in sports

The environment

Having more women in politics

Raising the speed limit in your state

Cloning

Government funding of controversial art

Abortion

Race relations

Building a school stadium that will raise tuition

The fur trade

Gun control

Capital punishment

Healthcare

The legalization of marijuana

Choose-One-of-Three Topics

Write a five-page essay in which you create an argument focusing on one of the following three topics: raising the minimum wage, government funding of controversial art, or universal healthcare.

Since we already have three possible topics, we need to think about which one we want to write on. A brainstorming chart can help you in your selection. Write the three topics on the left side of your sheet, with spaces in between. Write down your thoughts to the right of each topic.

Potential Topics for Essay

Topics	*Thoughts*
Raising minimum wage	– Income should adjust w/ economic growth
	– Infringes on American dream
	– Raising it would hurt small businesses
Government funding of controversial art	– A good source for public tax dollars?
	– Who decides what is controversial or not?
	– Controversy breeds innovation and change
	– If governement supports corporations, why not artists who need it
Universal healthcare	– HMOs won't perform some surgeries
	– Rich get better healthcare than poor

Predetermined Topic *Write a five-page essay in which you argue for or against a law that would allow religious head garb in driver's license photos.*

For an essay on a predetermined topic, you need only to come up with great thoughts on whatever topic was assigned. A chart is crucial. Be sure to record each of your thoughts carefully so you'll be able to determine which arguments work well and which don't. Leave enough space for ideas that stem from other ideas. You'll want to be able to follow your thinking process.

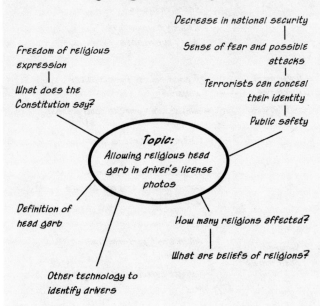

My Thoughts for Essay

Decrease in national security

Sense of fear and possible attacks

Terrorists can conceal their identity

Public safety

Freedom of religious expression

What does the Constitution say?

Topic:
Allowing religious head garb in driver's license photos

Definition of head garb

How many religions affected?

What are beliefs of religions?

Other technology to identify drivers

Narrow Your Choices

Once you've created your chart and have a group of possible topics or ideas, you're ready to think critically about which are mediocre and which really shine. You should follow four guidelines when figuring out which topics and ideas are viable options for your essay:

1. The topic or idea should have the potential for serious debate.
2. You should be able to argue both sides.
3. The topic or idea should inspire original thoughts and opinions.
4. The topic or idea should be unique.

In other words, a good topic or idea is important, arguable, inspiring, and unique. Cross off anything in your chart that doesn't meet these criteria.

Important Many students choose essay topics that practically write themselves—the risks of drinking and driving, the beauty of Renaissance art. What instructors want to see is your ability to grapple with difficult issues that demand analytical thought. You won't score any points on topics that are too easy to argue. Unsure whether your topic is important enough? Do the dinner-party test: if you and your friends could debate the topic heatedly over the course of a meal, your topic is worthy. If the conversation would peter out before you even finish your salads, you can bet the topic is too wishy-washy for your instructors.

If your topic is predetermined, ask yourself what makes the assigned topic important. Even if it doesn't seem important to you, answering this question will help you to see the topic through your instructor's eyes—and will lead you to write a better essay.

Arguable Though it seems counterintuitive, you should be able to argue both sides of your topic effectively. For example, if you absolutely love tangerines and can't fathom why anyone *doesn't* like them, it would be hard to imagine writing an effective essay about the greatness of tangerines. You're so biased that you can't argue persuasively:

> *Why not tangerines—they're juicy, flavorful, healthy, inexpensive, and delicious!*

Ultimate Style

It simply doesn't occur to you that someone might dislike the tangerine's size, color, taste, or numerous seeds. What you'd end up with would be a paper that *had no argument* because it *couldn't imagine an argument*. Strong arguments acknowledge the converse of their thesis and then prove it false—they don't ignore the converse altogether.

Make sure you're familiar with common viewpoints from both sides of the debate so that you'll have a multilayered perspective that will help you to write a more convincing essay. If your topic isn't open-ended, make sure you're able to argue both sides of the one that you've been assigned. If you're not, you're going to need to conduct a little research to discover some common viewpoints from the side of the debate you don't support or understand.

Argument in Action The strongest arguments acknowledge the converse of their thesis and then prove it false. Here's an excerpt from an essay that supports gun control that does this effectively:

While many opponents of gun control insist that a handgun
cannot kill someone without a person to pull its trigger, the fact
remains that cheaper and more accessible weapons such as
knives and blunt objects are responsible for far fewer homicides
each year than handguns. Clearly, the inherent power, ease of
use, and allure of handguns do in some way contribute to their
frequent use, despite the fact that they are loud, easy to trace
forensically, and require a permit for ownership.

Even if you don't agree with the point being made, this essay
is convincing because its author carefully considered divergent
opinions and then used them to strengthen his own argument.
In essence, he used his enemies' words against them.

Inspiring   Essays differ from research papers and tests in
that you're supposed to provide *your own thoughts and opinions*.
Instructors want your insights, beliefs, and unique views. While
it's perfectly acceptable to discuss things you learned in class
to demonstrate that you were paying attention, you must also
develop your own original thoughts and reasoning. By "inspiring," we don't mean the self-help-book variety of inspiration.
Rather, your topic should *inspire* insights and new ideas in both
you and your readers.

Developing new insights and unique views is difficult if
the subject you're studying doesn't inspire you, or if you don't
have any particularly original thoughts on it. For example, let's
say you get an open-ended prompt that asks for your thoughts
on Iceland. Iceland may not particularly intrigue you, so how
do you build up some passion for this topic? You've never even

thought about Iceland except that it sounds *chilly*. But if you do just a tad of research, you find that Iceland is one of the homes of the northern lights, a truly mysterious phenomenon that excites the budding astronomer in you. Suddenly an open-ended, seemingly bland topic is intriguing to you. You're *inspired*.

You should always do your best to get connected to your topic. Spend some quality time analyzing the topic to discover what it truly means to you and what effect it might have on your life. These thoughts will personalize your perspective, which will ultimately lead you to being inspired and interested in the topic.

Ultimate Style

Unique   Choosing a unique topic is tricky. What's fresh today may be common tomorrow, depending on technology, current events, and the political climate. And you shouldn't necessarily avoid issues you feel passionate about just because they're not brand-new. If you feel very strongly about topics such as abortion or capital punishment, then go for it. Your passion could make your essay rise above the pack. But keep in mind that many of your fellow classmates will likely write on exactly the same thing. If the essay topic is more open-ended, you might instead consider issues that are more "under the radar" and less familiar to your instructors.

If your instructor has chosen a topic on which the whole class must write, you don't need to worry about the topic being unique. However, you will have to put extra effort into good analytical and writing skills to help your paper stand out from the pack. And it goes without saying that your *thoughts* on the topic can be as unique as you are.

Note Your Thoughts

Once you've narrowed down the topics on your brainstorming chart, note your thoughts on the remaining topics. The notes you make at this stage will help you figure out exactly what topic you should choose for your essay, or what approach to take on an assigned topic.

For example, on our open-ended topic chart, you might add the following to the possible topic *raising the speed limit*:

> Raising the speed limit—Cuts down on travel time
> Higher mortality rate for accidents
> Danger to locals and pedestrians
> Effect on gas consumption?

Even though these thoughts may become the arguments of your essay, they don't have to be perfect or fully formed at this stage. You should just think of the best arguments for each topic. Notice that the last thought on the above topic has a question mark—you're not sure if there's a relationship, but it's something to consider. Also notice that there are arguments on both sides of the debate, which is a good sign, but it also means you'll have to choose which side to argue.

You may realize that there are some topics on which you have surprisingly few original thoughts. For instance, maybe you're opposed to *building a new stadium at school that will raise tuition*, but the only argument against it you can think of is "All students shouldn't have to pay for something only some enjoy." That's not enough for a well-developed essay. Use the opportunity to cross another topic off your list.

If your topic is predetermined, this step is the most important one in developing your brainstorming chart. Since you have to write on a given topic, your thoughts on the subject are the only ammunition you have. Spend sufficient time listing as many thoughts as possible.

Judge Uniqueness

Ultimate Style

You should evaluate the uniqueness and persuasiveness of your individual thoughts. Like a movie critic, you can use a star system (from one to four) to rate your own ideas. Looking back at your thoughts for *raising the speed limit*, you may decide that while the arguments are strong, they're not unique—anyone debating the issue would likely come up with the same ones. If that's the case, maybe this topic will get only three stars for its strength of ideas.

If your topic is predetermined, you won't be able to be unique. Everyone in the class is writing on the same topic. However, that doesn't mean your *thoughts* can't be unique and persuasive. Your thoughts are what will make your paper stand out. Be particularly diligent in ranking your thoughts with stars for both uniqueness and persuasiveness.

Shrink Your Focus

Imagine trying to write a brief research paper on sports. Not volleyball, swimming, or the long jump—just sports. *All* sports. As Google will tell you, there are far too many sports in the world, and far too many issues surrounding them, to ever cram into five, ten, or even twenty pages. Even if you were allowed to write on just one sport—say, soccer—you'd still have trouble explaining the rules, history, tournament schedule, and legendary players without finding yourself with a sizeable coffee-table book.

If your topic is too broad, your analysis will only skim the surface, resulting in an essay that's shallow and unfocused. You'll have no time for in-depth analysis. So how do you know when your topic is too broad? There are two things to consider: subtopics and subjectivity. This step generally applies only to open-ended assignments, since your instructor won't purposely assign overly broad topics if he or she is giving you a topic or giving you a choice of three.

Subtopics   To determine if a topic is too broad, turn your attention to the arguments and thoughts on your brainstorming chart. Look at each argument and try to determine if it could be a topic in and of itself. A topic within a topic is a *subtopic*: an issue that is a branch of the topic you've written down but that could actually be a whole topic in and of itself. If you spot any subtopics, your topic is likely too broad, and you'll

either need to cross it off the brainstorming chart or consider
a smaller topic. Here are two examples from our open-ended
topic chart:

TOO BROAD: *Race relations.* We know this topic is too broad for
a short essay because a subtopic is listed as an argument. Look
at the third argument listed: *affirmative action.* Affirmative
action is a *branch* of race relations—in other words, it's merely
one aspect of the larger issue of race relations. It's controversial, and it can be argued. You could devote a brief essay entirely
to the topic *affirmative action.* This is your signal that the topic
race relations is too broad.

JUST RIGHT: *Raising the minimum wage.* None of our three arguments (*the economy, the American dream, and small businesses*)
are branches of the minimum wage. In fact, the minimum wage is
a branch of all three. Furthermore, these arguments don't work
as topics because they're not *issues*—they're not concepts that
can be argued. Finally, apply the commonsense barometer: can
the issue of minimum wage be sufficiently addressed in a short
essay? Yes, more or less. This topic doesn't seem too broad.

Subjectivity   Subjectivity plays a role in deciding what
topics are too broad or too narrow. What one person sees as a
perfect subject for five pages of analysis, another might feel is
barely enough for two pages—or hard to cover in fifty. Unless
something seems glaringly broad, such as *sports,* your process
of narrowing your focus will depend in part on your own sense
of how you write, reason, and argue.

Revising Your Chart in Action   After narrowing down your choices, noting your thoughts, and judging uniqueness, your chart will be much more than just a list of ideas. Take a look at how we revised our brainstorming charts for each type of essay assignment:

Open-Ended Topic   Our lengthy list of topics becomes much shorter once we've noted our thoughts, thought about uniqueness, and figured out which topics are too broad and uninteresting. Our revised chart looks like this:

Potential Topics for Essay

Topics	Arguments	Strength
~~World Peace~~		
Raising minimum wage	– Income should adjust w/ economic growth – Infringes on American dream – Raising it would hurt small businesses	****
~~The use of steroids in sports~~		
~~The Environment~~		
~~Having more women in politics~~		
A proposal to raise the speed limit in your state	– Cuts down on travel time – Higher mortality rate for accidents – Danger to locals/pedestrians – Effect on gas consumption?	**

~~Cloning~~

Government
funding of
controversial
art

- A good source for public tax dollars?
- Who decides what is controversial or not?
- Controversy breeds innovation and change   ********
- If governement supports corporations, why not artists who need it

~~Abortion~~

Race
relations

- Discrimination encourages violence   ********
- In Constitution, all people created equal
- Affirmative action

**Ultimate
Style**

~~Building a school~~
~~Stadium that will~~
~~raise tuition~~

- Why all students pay for something that only some enjoy

~~The Fur Trade~~

Gun control

- If their is legislation on drugs, why not guns
- 2nd Amendment rights   *******
- Easier to buy guns than cigarettes

~~Capital~~
~~Punishment~~

Healthcare

- HMOs won't perform some surgeries
- Rich get better healthcare than poor   ******

The legalization
of marijuana

- Could help cancer patients
- Eliminate drug trafficking & violence
- Save billions on war on drugs   *******

Choose-One-of-Three Topics Even though the three topics you've been assigned are all appropriate according to your
instructor, remember that you must choose the one that you can
best argue. We've crossed out topics we don't find interesting

and recorded all the thoughts we have for each topic. With only three choices, we can't be unique—someone in class is going to write on the same topic we do—but we can still rate our arguments on the merits of their strength. We've focused on how strong we think our own arguments are for each topic. Our revised chart looks like this:

Potential Topics for Essay

Topics	Arguments	Strength
Raising minimum wage	– Income should adjust w/ economic growth – Infringes on American dream – Raising it would hurt small businesses	****
Government funding of controversial art	– A good source for public tax dollars? – Who decides what is controversial or not? – Controversy breeds innovation and change – If government supports corporations, why not artists who need it?	****
~~Universal Healthcare~~	– HMOs won't perform some surgeries – Rich get better healthcare than poor	**

Predetermined Topic   When revising a chart for a predetermined topic, we added more thoughts to those we already had, wrote down related thoughts, and noted where we might have to do a little research. We also rated our ideas for uniqueness. Our revised chart looks like this:

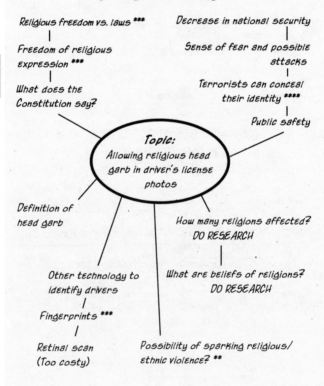

My Thoughts for Essay

Religious freedom vs. laws ***

Freedom of religious
expression ***

What does the
Constitution say?

Decrease in national security

Sense of fear and possible
attacks

Terrorists can conceal
their identity ****

Public safety

Topic:
Allowing religious head
garb in driver's license
photos

Definition of
head garb

How many religions affected?
DO RESEARCH

What are beliefs of religions?
DO RESEARCH

Other technology to
identify drivers

Fingerprints ***

Retinal scan
(Too costy)

Possibility of sparking religious/
ethnic violence? **

Make Your Choice

You have your chart, with all your careful notes and thoughts—now what? A brainstorming chart is a great tool, but it's not guaranteed to leave you with just one option. In the end, you may find you still have to make a final choice of what topic your essay will be about, or what approach you'll take to a predetermined topic. To decide on your final choice, take a close look at your brainstorming chart—you literally have your essay topic in your hands.

Final Choice: Open-Ended Topic   Once you've com-pleted all the steps in developing your chart, you may find that you still have more than one possible topic remaining. If you are left with two or more topics that seem more or less equally persuasive and unique, look at the number of arguments you've assigned to each. Choose the one with the most arguments. You could certainly come up with additional arguments for the other topics, but the ideas that first pop into your head are likely the best indicator of your enthusiasm for a topic.

In our revised chart, raising the minimum wage and government funding of controversial art both have four-star ratings for persuasiveness and uniqueness. Therefore, it's best to look at the number of arguments assigned to each. Since controversial art has more arguments, this is likely the best choice.

Final Choice: Choose-One-of-Three Topics As you may now realize, the choose-one-of-three topic is in many ways the essay with the least pressure. Even though you don't have the freedom to choose any topic you like, at least you're assured you won't choose a topic that's too broad, and uniqueness isn't an issue. However, your brainstorming chart has still enabled you to narrow selections based on your notion of what's inspiring, arguable, and important.

On our revised chart, universal healthcare has been crossed out because you have few thoughts with little strength. You're left with raising the minimum wage and government funding for controversial art, both of which have four stars. Just as you do with an open-ended topic, you should choose the one for which you have the most arguments: government funding for controversial art.

Ultimate Style

Final Choice: Predetermined Topic With predetermined topics, your goal in creating a brainstorming chart has not been to narrow topics down but to come up with as many thoughts as possible about the topic you've been given. The thoughts you jot down will become your arguments, reasons, and examples when you begin creating a thesis and outline. When you decide what approach to take to your assigned topic, see what ideas are linked. When you notice a trend, you can create a thesis statement around this idea. In our revised chart, you can see that the idea of "freedom of religious expression" is an underlying idea for many other ideas on the chart, so we'll create a thesis that deals with this element of the topic.

When you look at your revised chart, you'll see that not all of your thoughts will have resulted in solid arguments yet. Some may just be questions to consider, and others may require some research. This should be noted when appropriate so you'll be reminded of the work that may have to be done to arrive at a sufficient number of convincing arguments. If you come up with thoughts that prove not to be appropriate or supportive of your debate, don't erase them or scribble them out so they are illegible. These thoughts may later provide you with good counterarguments when you develop reasoning and examples.

Let Us Show You

In this book, we're going to create an essay right along with you to show you how the things we're saying play out in a real-life essay. We're going to write our essay on the topic *government funding of controversial art*, which we chose for an open-ended essay assignment. You've seen us brainstorm to choose this topic—and now we'll take this topic with us into the chapters that follow as we create a thesis, develop arguments, outline, and, finally, write the essay.

Creating the Thesis

Once you have a topic for your essay, you can't just sit down and start writing haphazardly about it—your random thoughts on a subject might interest your cat or your smitten significant other, but they won't do much in the way of helping you write a good essay. Instead, you have to develop a specific, original idea about your topic, an idea around which your entire essay will revolve. This idea is called your *thesis statement*.

A thesis statement is a bit like a movie preview. A movie preview must represent a film accurately so that the audience knows what to expect. If someone expects a comedy and instead winds up watching a tearful drama, he or she will leave the theater disappointed and annoyed. Your thesis statement, too, must accurately represent your essay. It prepares readers for the *tone*, *subject matter*, and *content* they're about to encounter. To create a good thesis statement, you have to consider your topic carefully and decide exactly what you want to argue.

Define "Thesis"   Take a look at the definition
of a thesis from *Merriam-Webster's Collegiate Dictionary*:

> **THESIS** the • sis *n*
> A position or proposition that a person (as a candidate for
> scholastic honors) advances and offers to maintain by argument

Let's translate. A thesis is a clear, concise, and unambiguous declaration of what your opinion is on the topic you're discussing. In other words, a thesis isn't the topic itself; a thesis is your *opinion* on the topic. If your essay is about book banning (your topic), your thesis is your *opinion* on book banning, such as that libraries should be able to ban books according to the librarians' personal values. Your essay will argue that point.

Weak and Flawed Theses   An argument is only as good as its thesis—and since an essay is little more than a written argument, an essay, too, is only as good as its thesis. If you have

a weak thesis, you won't be able to write a good essay, no matter how coherent your examples and reasoning are. And sometimes a thesis isn't just weak—it's simply wrong. Take a look at this example:

> In The Plague, *Albert Camus creates an extended metaphor for the Vietnam War.*

No matter how long or passionately you argued this thesis, you'd never convince your readers of anything, for one important reason: the book predated the war by twenty years. Unless Camus had been psychic, he couldn't have created a metaphor for a war that hadn't yet been fought. If you have a fundamentally flawed thesis, it doesn't matter how well you write, argue, or reason. Make sure you have your facts straight when you create your thesis.

Requirements for a Successful Thesis   A successful thesis statement meets four requirements:

1. It appears near the beginning of the essay (no more than 10 percent of the way in).
2. It is as succinct as possible—no longer than three sentences.
3. It is explicit and clear.
4. It doesn't mention anything that the essay doesn't explain later.

These four rules for thesis statements are universal for all kinds of essays. Figuring out what constitutes 10 percent isn't difficult. If you're writing a two-page essay, your thesis should appear close to the beginning of the first page. If you're writing a five-page essay, your thesis should appear no later than half a page in. And so on. Just remember that the bulk of your essay should be the argument that proves that your thesis makes sense.

Thesis in Action   "On the Duty of Civil Disobedience" (1849) by Henry David Thoreau is one of the most famous essays ever written. Thoreau argues that it is every citizen's duty to act according to their morals, even if that conflicts with what the government dictates. He begins his essay with these now-famous words:

> I heartily accept the motto, "That government is best which governs least"; and I should like to see it acted up to more rapidly and systematically. Carried out, it finally amounts to this, which also I believe—"That government is best which governs not at all"; and when men are prepared for it, that will be the kind of government which they will have.

No thesis yet. Thoreau is simply grounding his readers in his *topic*: the role of government. While he expresses an opinion, it's just his own take on a famous "motto." It isn't until later, in his fourth paragraph, that he provides us with his thesis:

> But, to speak practically and as a citizen, unlike those who call themselves no-government men, I ask for, not at once no government, but at once a better government. Let every man make known what kind of government would command his respect, and that will be one step toward obtaining it.

Ultimate Style

Thoreau makes his message clear: he supports the idea of government (he's not an anarchist), but he also believes in a *better* government, which can be achieved by various means of protest. While he proceeds to discuss history, theorize on the role of government, and provide examples of his own protest against taxation, everything connects back to this succinct thesis statement.

Thoreau fully adheres to the four main rules for a successful thesis. His thesis statement is short, it comes early (about 5 percent of the way into his nearly 9,500-word essay), it makes his opinion clear, and it doesn't mention anything the essay doesn't explain later.

Be Opinionated

When you say someone is opinionated, it's probably not a compliment. You usually mean that person is stubborn, stridently vocal, and unrelenting in his or her convictions—in short, not someone you'd want to be stranded on a desert island with. But the rules for essay success are different: an opinionated thesis is a must. Since a thesis *is* an opinion, it can't be "right" or "wrong," but it can definitely be strong or weak. Instructors are looking for a thesis that presents a bold idea. Remember these two guidelines:

1. A strong thesis is opinionated. It takes a firm stance on an issue, supports it fervently, and refuses to equivocate.
2. A wishy-washy thesis has no opinion; it's not quite sure which side it stands on, and it speaks quietly, as if afraid to be heard.

You can always explore the nuances and gray areas of an issue even if your thesis is strong. You might, for example, be adamantly pro-choice on the abortion issue *with exceptions* (such as third-trimester abortions). You might be anti-capital punishment *with exceptions* (such as in the case of terrorism). You don't have to choose just one extreme or the other—you just have to make sure you're *passionate* about whatever stance you choose. The more specific you are in brainstorming and formulating arguments, the more likely you are to reach a thesis that is strong but considerate of all the given options.

Your Instructor's Views You might worry that if your instructor doesn't agree with your opinion (thesis), he or she may give you a lower grade. But in general, instructors respect divergent opinions. As much as they want students to learn from their classes, they also want to foster individuality and uniqueness. In essays, they want to see solid arguments, strong reasoning, analytical thought, and good writing skills. If you manage to use these elements to successfully argue a case your instructor doesn't agree with, he or she won't hold it against you. In fact, many instructors are impressed with students who are bold enough to disagree with concepts the instructors obviously espouse or oppose.

Ultimate Style

One tip: don't be disrespectful with your choices. It's one thing to argue that Joan Miró is a better surrealist that Salvador Dali, even if you know your art history instructor loves Dali. It's another thing to devote your entire paper to this thesis: "Salvador Dali is an inept imbecile, and anyone who likes him has either had a lobotomy or needs one immediately."

Choose a Side

Most people think they should choose to argue the side they personally agree with—but this can actually be a mistake. Think back to the essay topic from Chapter 2, *building a new stadium that will raise tuition*. Let's say you're against the proposed stadium, but the only reasoning you can come up with is that it isn't fair for all students to pay for something that only a handful get to use. However, there are plenty of arguments in *favor* of the stadium: the current stadium is in disrepair; the school could attract more and better athletes; more ticket sales would benefit the school in the long run; and school pride could soar. To successfully argue your side of the debate, you'll have to disprove every one of these arguments—a lengthy proposition. It makes more sense to argue the opposing side, rather than the one you personally support.

As this example shows, argument is even more important than opinion. Remember this rule: it's the arguments you use to support your thesis, rather than the side you are personally, emotionally, or instinctively drawn to, that best determines what side of the issue to argue. Before you can choose a side, you'll have to come up with arguments for both sides of your debate—a task your brainstorming chart can help with.

Revisit Your Chart

To determine which side of a debate to choose for your thesis, go back to your brainstorming chart. Here are the arguments we wrote down for *government funding for controversial art*:

- A good source for public tax dollars?
- Who decides what is controversial or not?
- Controversy breeds innovation and change.
- If government supports corporations, why not artists who need it?

These ideas seem pretty crude, but remember, we were just brainstorming. The next step is to rewrite these arguments so that they're more keenly developed. If you're writing on a predetermined topic, write out your ideas so that they're more fully formed. They still don't need to be grammatically perfect or written beautifully—you should focus instead on developing ideas more fully. They might look like this:

- Public tax money shouldn't be spent on art that only a small percentage of taxpayers actually see.
- A democratic government should not determine what constitutes "good" and "bad" art, nor what is and isn't "obscene."
- Much of the most influential and innovative art was once considered controversial.
- The government gives millions to large, profitable corporations; it should also assist emerging artists and foster cultural awareness.

Now we have four solid arguments. In addition, we thought of two more as we studied the chart and rewrote our original arguments:

- If the government legislates fine art, will they start censoring films, music, TV shows, and other artistic entertainment?
- "Obscene" art might discourage some from going to museums.

Not all of these arguments will necessarily make it into the essay, and in Chapter 4 we'll discuss in more detail how to develop and select the best arguments to make your case.

But for now, let's divide the arguments according to which side of the debate they support:

Arguments on Government Funding for Controversial Art

PRO

1. A democratic government should not determine what constitutes "good" and "bad" art, nor what is and isn't "obscene."

2. Much of the most influential and innovative art was once considered controversial.

3. The government gives to profitable corporations; it should also assist artists and foster cultural awareness.

4. If the government legislates fine art, will they start censoring films, music, TV shows, and other artistic entertainment?

CON

1. Public tax money shouldn't be spent on art that only a small percentage of taxpayers actually see.

2. "Obscene" art might discourage some from going to museums.

Since there are more arguments on the Pro than the Con side, we should probably go with the Pro side. But just to be safe, you should evaluate your arguments a second way. You should try to see if you can create counterarguments that refute the side for which you have fewer arguments.

Creating Counterarguments To create counterarguments, you should examine the potential arguments that could weaken or even refute the side you've chosen to argue. You don't want to leave any holes in your own argument where readers might be able to point out a flaw or weakness.

1. Public tax money shouldn't be spent on art that only a small percentage of tax payers actually see.

But . . .

• Public tax dollars are often used to fund things that only a few benefit from, such as farm subsidies and financing the construction of professional sports stadiums and arenas.

2. "Obscene" art might discourage some from going to museums.

But . . .

• Controversy usually attracts public attention. Furthermore, there are plenty of resources for more traditional, classical art for more conservative tastes.

In this case, we could find a way to argue with both Con arguments. This means that when you write your essay, you'll be able to address the Con side and refute the arguments that support it, which will strengthen your own Pro position. Counterarguments will strengthen your thesis.

Write the Thesis

You have a topic, you've chosen a side to debate, you have your arguments and counterarguments, and you know the rules—you're ready to write a thesis statement. Do *not* start outlining or drafting your essay until you write your thesis statement! Always write your thesis statement first. There are two reasons to do so:

1. You'll need to have a solid, focused thesis before you outline your essay. This will help you configure your outline and order your examples and reasoning.

2. The thesis is the hub of your essay, from which everything else flows. If there's a flaw in your thesis, better to discover it now than after you've written numerous pages.

Take a look at this thesis statement for our essay on government funding for controversial art:

> By ceasing to fund art that some feel is controversial, the government would stifle creative innovation, overstep its boundaries by endorsing only state-approved art, and ultimately set a dangerous precedent for censorship of other artistic mediums such as film and music.

We've carefully chosen our side, so we can confidently take a firm stance on it. We've already decided what arguments we'll use to support our thesis, which means we can incorporate that logic into our statement. And finally, this thesis statement adheres to all the rules:

- It's short.
- It's clear.
- It doesn't mention concepts we're unprepared to discuss later.
- And we'll make sure to put it near the beginning of our essay.

Notice that while our thesis is on the Pro side of the issue (we *want* governments to fund controversial art), the thesis statement has been worded as a Con argument (we *don't* want governments to cut such funding). This is often a wise strategy: it creates a sense of urgency and drama by reminding readers of impending changes or restrictions, rather than just suggesting that things are fine as they are and will stay that way.

Keep in mind: your thesis statement isn't finished until your essay is. Even if you write it early on, it's not set in stone. You may have to reword it to fit more smoothly with your essay's introduction. You may come up with a really good example later on in the writing process and wish to incorporate it into the thesis. By giving the thesis statement some flexibility, your essay will develop more naturally because you won't feel trapped.

Developing Arguments

This is where the true challenge of essay writing begins: finding a way to argue your thesis and convince your readers that you're right. To do this, you have to show your readers why your thesis makes sense—in other words, you must provide *reasons* that show why you're right. And to illustrate those reasons, you must give *examples*. Your reasons and examples are the heart of your essay—without them, you have no argument.

When you chose your topic and created your thesis, you took the first steps in finding reasons to support your argument—in fact, you wrote some reasons down in your brainstorming chart. But when it comes to creating a great argument, quality, not quantity, is what counts. You may be able to come up with one hundred reasons to support your argument, but not all of those reasons are going to be equally effective. Selecting reasons carefully is the key to creating an essay that blows your readers away.

Define the Terms

Reasoning and examples are what arguments are made of. You've surely heard the terms *reasoning* and *examples* in your everyday life, but when you're talking about essay writing, they have very distinct meanings:

- Reasoning: an abstract process of logic, analysis, and deduction. While reasoning may contain some concrete facts, its persuasive power depends on making logical connections that your audience can follow.
- Examples: the proof behind the reasoning. Examples are tangible, concrete, and often historical pieces of evidence that support your reasoning with commonly held beliefs or irrefutable facts.

You use reasoning and examples in everyday conversation. Let's say you're trying to convince a friend that *The Matrix* is

Ultimate Style

an excellent film. To convince him, you need reasons. You have one reason for believing *The Matrix* is excellent: the film is fast-paced. But the reason alone isn't enough. You need to show how the film is fast-paced and why being fast-paced is good. To prove that *The Matrix* is fast-paced, you might provide examples of all the action scenes and plot twists that occur in the first fifteen minutes. To show why being fast-paced is good, you could remind your friend of how he fell asleep during *The Long, Sad Life of Bingus Barbie*, but not during *The Matrix*—only the fast-paced film kept his attention.

As you can see, reasoning and examples are interdependent—they rely on each other to form an effective argument. Reasoning without examples is nothing more than conjecture, and examples need reasoning to have purpose. To write a successful essay, you need to present a number of arguments to support your thesis, and each argument will be composed of reasoning and examples.

Identify Your Purpose

Before you begin searching for appropriate reasoning and clear examples to support your argument, you should identify the *purpose* of your essay. Why are you writing it? In an academic essay, you'll do one of three things:

1. Convince
2. Persuade
3. Analyze

While all essays must contain arguments to support a thesis, the nature and presentation of the reasons and examples you select will vary according to your essay's specific purpose.

Essays That Convince   In an essay to convince, your goal is to argue a position or make a claim and get readers to both listen to and agree with you. You write essays to convince when your subject is "intellectual"—for example, when you're writing about a scientific, technical, or academic topic. Your opinion must be rational and supported by evidence. Our essay on government funding for controversial art is an essay to convince.

Essays That Persuade   Persuasive essays usually appear in courses focused on social, political, or value-based studies, such as sociology and political science. The goal of these essays is to persuade your audience on an emotional level that they must support your stance on an issue. You'll need to use logical reasoning and examples, but these reasons and examples must tap into your audience's common sense, values, and belief systems in order to be persuasive. Ultimately, the purpose of these essays is not just to convince your audience that your claim is correct but to persuade them to change their minds and take a specific course of action.

Essays That Analyze   Analytical essays are most often assigned in literature, art history, and philosophy courses. The goal is to answer a question about a specific text or artistic work, which you do by analyzing and interpreting the work and then illuminating the author's or artist's intentions. Analytical essays require reasoning that stems directly from the work you're analyzing and examples that reside within it.

Ultimate Style

Find Reasons on Your Chart

To find reasons to support your thesis, think about why you feel passionate about your subject and why you chose to argue a specific side of a debate. Take a look at your brainstorming chart—it's teeming with potential reasons. Your chart is where you recorded your thoughts on your topic, and these thoughts will serve as an excellent starting point for developing reasoning. Here are our thoughts for our essay on government funding of controversial art:

Pro Government Funding

- A democratic government should not determine what constitutes "good" and "bad" art, nor what is and isn't "obscene."
- Much of the most influential and innovative art was once considered controversial.
- The government gives millions to large, profitable corporations; it should also assist emerging artists and foster cultural awareness.
- If the government legislates fine art, will they start censoring films, music, TV shows, and other artistic entertainment?

Con Government Funding (with Counterarguments)

- Public tax money shouldn't be spent on art that only a small percentage of taxpayers actually see (*but* public tax dollars are often used to fund things that only a few benefit from, such as farm subsidies and financing professional sports stadiums and arenas).
- "Obscene" art might discourage some from going to museums (*but* controversy usually attracts public attention. Furthermore, there are plenty of resources for more traditional, classical art for more conservative tastes).

All of these thoughts are reasons that support our argument. Your work isn't over—these are simply preliminary reasons, and you'll need to look further. Keep them in mind as you continue looking for reasons.

Look for Deeper Reasons

Simply gathering preliminary reasons from your chart and turning them into an essay isn't an effective way to build a convincing case. You should spend some time looking for more reasons and then figuring out which reasons are most convincing for your essay.

Ultimate Style

Where can you find reasons? There are six places to look:

1. Definition
2. Comparison and consistency
3. Tradition and custom
4. Values
5. Likelihood and hypothetical probability
6. Evidence and history

You should use this list to help you come up with new reasons, as well as to classify and better understand the reasons you already have from your chart. When writing an essay, you don't have to draw reasons from every category; not all categories will be suitable for all essays. The real benefit of this list is to inspire new thoughts and ideas. We've provided explanations of each category and shown how the reasons from our chart fit into them.

Definition   Consider the textbook or dictionary definition of the issue you're discussing. You may find that you can support your thesis by directing your audience's attention to the technical definition of the issue. Conversely, you may find a word has been consistently defined incorrectly by opponents of your issue—reasoning that may convince your audience that they've been duped.

Argument in Action   Finding reasons through definition:
Reasoning that the definition of "controversial" is not "bad" but rather "provoking disagreement" may persuade your audience to see that controversial art is not necessarily "obscene," and that many government-sponsored programs are indeed controversial.

Comparison and Consistency   By comparing the issue you're discussing to one with similar values or beliefs at stake, you may convince your audience that to object to/support one issue and not another would be hypocritical. You may also be able to reason that your stance is consistent with widely held beliefs on similar issues.

Argument in Action   Finding reasons through comparison and consistency:
The reasoning "If the government legislates fine art, will they start censoring films, music, TV shows, and other artistic entertainment?" is a form of comparison. Since your audience would likely oppose the government deciding what TV shows they can watch, you can reason that they should oppose the government deciding what art they can view.

The reasoning "The government gives millions to large, profitable corporations; it should also assist emerging artists and foster cultural awareness" uses consistency to reason in favor of your thesis. When your audience considers what the government does spend money on, they may be more likely to feel that art is also worth the cost.

Tradition and Custom   People are generally proud of their customs and eager to uphold their traditions—a fact you should exploit whenever possible. By reasoning that your stance is in keeping with tradition, you'll appeal to people on an emotional level and show that there is a precedent for your thinking. You could also point to a flawed or archaic tradition (such as witch-burning or slavery) to create parallels, reasoning that the status quo must change. This type of reason works most effectively when readers are familiar with and respectful of the tradition or custom you are drawing from.

Argument in Action   Finding reasons through tradition and custom:

The counterargument that "Public tax dollars are often used to fund things that only a few benefit from, such as farm subsidies and the construction of professional sports stadiums and arenas" makes use of tradition for its reasoning. (However, you may now realize that there is a problem with this line of reasoning—many people loathe paying taxes and feel it's a tradition that needs reform.)

Values   Individuals, communities, cultures, and countries have specific values that determine many of their opinions and beliefs. Equality, liberty, justice, and freedom are all examples of values that people tend to hold dear. Reasoning that your stance is in accordance with widely held values will both convince and persuade.

Argument in Action   Finding reasons through values:

Two reasons from our brainstorming chart appeal to democratic values: "A democratic government should not determine what constitutes 'good' and 'bad' art, nor what is and isn't 'obscene'," and "If the government legislates fine art, will they start censoring films, music, TV shows, and other artistic entertainment?"

These reasons are both value based, and they both address the same issue: censorship. Instead of having them as two separate reasons, consider linking them together into one, more encompassing reason addressing the idea of censorship: "If a government supports some art while rejecting other art, it is in essence practicing censorship—the bane of a democratic system." By figuring out what type of reasons you have, you can avoid redundancy and create more nuanced reasons.

Likelihood and Hypothetical Probability   Reasoning that falls into this category is very powerful when carefully thought through. This form of reasoning envisions a probable future that is likely to become reality if changes are or are not implemented. By engaging your audience's imagination and logic, you can present a future that is either reprehensible if your stance is not espoused, or utopian if your stance is embraced. You can use this type of reasoning when arguing for or against a proposed plan or idea, or when you're defending or opposing one possible account of events.

Argument in Action   Finding reasons through likelihood and hypothetical probability:

"If the government legislates fine art, will they start censoring films, music, TV shows, and other artistic entertainment?" is hypothetical probability. You are indicating what may occur if your stance is not embraced by your audience.

We could also draw this reason from comparison and consistency—sometimes reasons are rooted in more than one of these categories. They can overlap.

Evidence and History   Most people find it difficult *not* to believe cold, hard facts and proven history, and using these in your essay will lend authenticity and legitimacy to your reasoning. You can also use evidence and history as support when your own experiences are insufficient.

Argument in Action   Finding reasons through evidence and history:

"Much of the most influential and innovative art was once considered controversial" is history-based reasoning. To prove this point, you'll have to supply actual examples of controversial yet innovative art, but the reasoning itself is sound and convincing. The counterarguments "Controversy usually attracts public attention" and "There are plenty of resources for more traditional, classical art for more conservative tastes" are reasons that will also need examples later on.

Select Appropriate Reasons

Once you've come up with reasons that support your thesis, you need to decide which reasons to include in your essay. Not all reasons will work all the time. As good as your reasons might be on their own, they won't help your essay if they don't serve your specific purpose. You must carefully examine each reason you come up with to make sure it is appropriate for your essay. Consider the type of essay you're writing when you're deciding what reasons are appropriate:

- For an essay to convince, you should use reasons based on definition, comparison, likelihood or probability, and evidence. These appeal most to the logic and rationality of your audience.
- For a persuasive essay, you might also include reasons based on traditions and customs and values. These appeal to the "whole person" of your readers, not just their intellect.
- For an analytical essay, you can include reasons based on definition, comparison, and evidence, but most of your reasons will come from the text itself.

Find Examples

Reasoning without examples is merely conjecture, so you'll need to come up with at least one example for every reason you include. More complex reasoning may require numerous examples to be convincing. When searching for examples that support your reasoning, you'll need to revisit each reason and then come up with a tangible, factual, or historical example.

Examples in Action   Every argument consists of reasons and examples. Let's look at some of our reasons for our essay on government funding of controversial art and figure out what examples might support them:

> If a government supports some art while rejecting other art, it is in essence practicing censorship—the bane of a democratic system.

- A good example might be a comparison to Communist China, which censors art it deems improper.

We created this reason from two other reasons:

> A democratic government should not determine what constitutes "good" and "bad" art, nor what is and isn't "obscene."

> If the government legislates fine art, will they start censoring films, music, TV shows, and other artistic entertainment?

These are now supporting reasons, and we can explore them
for further examples:

- One example could be based on the definition of "good"
  art: "If a government starts classifying good art as classical
  landscapes and bad art as nude sketches, what's to stop it
  from classifying pro-government art as good, and anything
  that expresses criticism of the government as bad?"
- We can consider a hypothetical situation as an example:
  "Since TV shows such as *The Sopranos* and *The Simpsons*
  are considered controversial to some, this trend might lead
  to the government censoring these shows as well."

A fairly complex and thorough line of reasoning has been
developed, with a major reason supported by an example,
as well as two supporting reasons, also supported by specific
examples. Here's another reason:

> *Much of the most influential and innovative art was once
> considered controversial.*

- This historical reasoning requires a historical example. You
  might start by thinking of controversial yet influential artists, such as Pablo Picasso, Francis Bacon, and Andy Warhol.
- If you're not terribly familiar with fine art, think of
  comparison-based examples such as The Beatles, a greatly
  influential band that generated much controversy for
  statements and lyrics about religion and drugs. Other pop
  culture references might also be appropriate (such as rap
  music, or the films of Quentin Tarantino or Spike Lee).

Conducting Research   If you find you're having difficulty coming up with examples to support your reasoning, you may have to conduct some research. In this case, a book on art history will likely provide you with names of controversial artists, as well as anecdotal examples of public reaction or government intervention. Searching the web for "controversial art" may turn up examples as well. A text used in your course may also have examples. In general, however, examples were likely in the back of your mind when you thought up reasons. For example, how else would you have known that most innovative art was once considered controversial? It's usually just a matter of time before you can pinpoint the examples behind the reasoning.

Ultimate Style

Outlining

Outlines are essentially road maps that organize your thoughts into a cohesive, structured whole. Outlines aren't just helpful; they're crucial. During the preparation process, you gathered ideas, thoughts, reasons, and examples that you thought would build an effective essay. But you can't just toss them all together and assume they'll make sense. You need to carefully arrange them, see how they fit together, and eliminate anything that doesn't seem logical, relevant, or effective.

When you have your road map—your outline—in front of you, you'll know exactly what to include in your essay, and in what order. If you feel panicked at the sight of a blank computer screen, an outline will be your lifesaver. If you start out with a strong plan for how to organize your essay logically, when it's time to write your first draft you can focus on the actual *writing*. Spending time on your outline will make writing a first draft immeasurably easier.

Break Down the Structure

An essay is made up of three main parts:

1. A simple and coherent thesis statement
2. Examples and reasoning to support the thesis statement
3. A conclusion that summarizes all of this information

In the outlining process, this basic structure gets broken down further to include all the individual elements that comprise an essay. Here, we give you a generic outline that can work no matter what kind of essay you're writing, whether it's an SAT essay or a twenty-page essay. Keep in mind that you won't always have three supporting arguments in the body of your essay. You may have more or fewer, depending on how long your essay is. Also, one supporting argument is not necessary one paragraph in your essay—an argument may very well stretch out over several paragraphs.

I. INTRODUCTION

A. Introducing your topic

B. Your thesis statement

C. Introducing your arguments (optional)

II. BODY

A. First major supporting argument

  1. Transition and introduction

  2. Reasoning and examples

  3. Argument conclusion

B. Second major supporting argument

  1. Transition and introduction

  2. Reasoning and examples

  3. Argument conclusion

C. Third major supporting argument

    1. Transition and introduction

    2. Reasoning and examples

    3. Argument conclusion

III. CONCLUSION

A. Transition to thesis restatement

B. Summary of arguments

C. A new perspective or future idea

Like the structure, the outline is divided into three parts—one for the introduction and thesis, one for supporting arguments, and one for the conclusion. The **introduction** is used to orient your readers. It informs them what topic you'll be discussing and what your opinion on it is. It makes up about 10 percent of your essay. The **body** is the meat of the essay. Here, you'll back up your thesis with supporting arguments, which will be divided into reasoning and examples. This will be the longest part of your essay (about 75–90 percent). In the **conclusion**, you'll summarize everything presented thus far and tie it together for a final persuasive punch. Your conclusion will make up about 5–10 percent of your essay.

When you outline, you don't have to worry about writing out the transition and introduction of each argument—you'll do this when you write the first draft. You may be able to write a basic conclusion to each argument, based on the reasoning and examples you put into your outline, but remember that this will be only a basic attempt. The point of outlining is to *organize* your thoughts so that you'll be ready to write later on.

Organize Your Arguments

For the most part, the outline is like a mathematical formula: once you know and understand it, you just plug in the variables and you're ready to roll. There is one task that requires some thought and careful consideration, however: organizing your supporting arguments to be as logical, convincing, and persuasive as possible.

A Lesson from Law   Lawyers are pros at making convincing arguments—and outlines are key to their success. You've seen in movies and on TV how lawyers introduce evidence and witnesses to make their case. What you may not know is how carefully lawyers organize the *order* in which they introduce these "supporting arguments."

Imagine you're on a jury for a murder case, and the prosecutor has three key pieces of evidence to prove the defendant, John Doe, is guilty:

1. Fingerprints on the gun
2. A taped phone conversation in which he bragged about the crime
3. A ninety-six-year-old witness who saw John Doe from her window before the shooting

If the first argument introduced was the ninety-six-year-old lady, you and your fellow jurors would probably start off as somewhat skeptical. An ancient lady with thick glasses peering out into the nighttime isn't the most credible witness. Even though the fingerprints and phone conversation are introduced a few days later, the prosecution has to work hard now to convince you, because you started off dubious. The prosecutor made the mistake of starting with the weakest argument. Had he started with the fingerprints or the phone conversation, you'd be convinced from the beginning, and the rest (credible and not-so-credible) would just be icing on the cake.

The simple lesson: arrange your supporting arguments in order of strongest to weakest. This way, you'll be sure to get your readers on your side from the outset, which will lessen the burden of convincing later on.

Logic   Arranging arguments logically is key in convincing and persuading your readers. Try to put yourself in the minds of your readers: what argument could you present early on that would strengthen the conviction of one provided later? If there is a chronology inherent to your argument (a timetable of events, history, or story), try to arrange your arguments in chronological order, which will aid your readers in understanding the cause and effect of your issue. If one argument follows logically from another, try to place it directly after the first—separating related thoughts, even by just a paragraph, will cause you to sacrifice the logical momentum you want to create in the minds of your readers.

In the murder case, we know the ninety-six-year-old woman is the weakest argument, so she'll go last. But if you can't decide which is stronger between the fingerprints and John Doe's confession, think logically. Would the jury be more convinced by the confession before or after knowing hard evidence exists? They'd probably be more convinced afterward, because they'd already have a mental image of the fingerprints on the gun. If the confession was the first argument introduced, the jury might not take it as seriously, because they wouldn't yet know if there was any other way to prove John Doe was on the scene.

Placing Counterarguments   You should never use a counterargument as the first argument in your essay, even if you feel it's compelling, because counterarguments require you to acknowledge opposing views. You'd essentially be starting off an essay showing how you might be proven wrong. Counterarguments ultimately strengthen your essay, but you should get your audience on your side of the debate before giving any credence to other viewpoints. Going back to our fictitious murder trial, imagine if the prosecution began their case with the argument, "It's true that John Doe's fingerprints on the murder weapon doesn't prove he actually pulled the trigger. However, since there are no other prints on the gun, he must have done it." Right from the beginning, you're skeptical: the lawyer hasn't yet established credibility, and already he's introducing doubt.

Ultimate Style

Arrange Reasons and Examples

Once you've decided the order in which to present your arguments, you should next proceed inward, arranging the reasons and examples within each argument. Much of this process has already been achieved in previous steps, when you decided what your reasons were and came up with appropriate examples. Now, you'll want to use logic to arrange these reasons and examples in the most convincing way possible.

After looking over our reasoning in our developing essay, we may decide that "If a government supports some art while rejecting other art, it is in essence practicing censorship—the bane of a democratic system" is our strongest argument. It's broad and sweeping, logically informs our other reasoning, and has strength in its appeal to fundamental American values. After arranging the reasoning and examples within this argument, we arrive at something like this:

First Major Supporting Argument

- If a government supports some art while rejecting other art, it is in essence practicing censorship—the bane of a democratic system.

Transition and Introduction (We'll write this later.)

Reasons and Examples

- Freedom of expression is a cherished value in a democracy (reason).
  - Art in Communist China (example)
- Democracies shouldn't determine the value of art (reason).
  - Subjective nature of art, styles, and forms (examples)
  - Is a landscape "good" and nude "bad"? (example)
- This practice could lead to political suppression of art (reason).

- — Allowing politically positive art, stifling art of dissent (example)
- This paves the way for censorship of other forms of art (reason).
  - — Favorite TV shows, films, music (examples)

Argument Conclusion (a rough attempt)

- If we allow our government to dictate what arts is and isn't acceptable, we compromise our democracy, opening the doors for further censorship.

Ultimate Style

Examples and reasoning have been logically woven together to inform one another, ultimately leading to a persuasive concluding argument. When you write your essay, you won't divide examples and reasoning so deliberately. They may even be incorporated into the same sentences. However, understanding their interrelated nature will help you create a logical development in your outline. You'll use this same process to complete the outline for the entire essay.

Outlining in Action   A completed outline involves figuring out what arguments to use to build your case, what reasons and examples are most appropriate and convincing, and how all the pieces connect together to form a strong, relevant conclusion. Here's our outline for our essay on government funding for controversial art:

Outline for Essay on Controversial Art

I. INTRODUCTION

A. Introduce controversial art, history, impending crisis

B. Thesis statement

C. Introducing your arguments (optional)

II. BODY

A. First Major Supporting Argument: If a government supports some art while rejecting other art, it is in essence practicing censorship—the bane of a democratic system.

    1. Transition and Introduction

    2. Reasons and Examples

      a. Freedom of expression is a cherished value in a democracy (reason).

        – Art in Communist China (example)

      b. Democracies shouldn't determine the value of art (reason).

        – Subjective nature of art, styles, and forms (examples)

        – Is a landscape "good" and nude "bad"? (example)

      c. This practice could lead to political suppression of art (reason).

        – Allowing politically positive art, stifling art of dissent (example)

    d. This paves the way for censorship of other
forms of art (reason).
  - Favorite TV shows, films, music: *The
Simpsons, The Sopranos, Fahrenheit
9/11,* Eminem, (examples)

  3. Argument Conclusion: If we allow our government to dictate what art is and isn't acceptable,
we compromise our democracy, opening the
doors for further censorship.

B. Second Major Supporting Argument: Arts funding is not only consistent with other forms of public
funding, but its dissolution would jeopardize the
future of American art

  1. Transition and Introduction

  2. Reasons and Examples

    a. Though some may argue arts funding is
frivolous, the government consistently
supports programs that benefit communities
(reason).
  - Taxes fund farm subsidies, construction
of sports stadiums and arenas, education (examples)

    b. The government even gives millions to
profitable corporations; why not artists who
barely scrape by (reason)?
  - Art receives small fraction of money for
corporations (example)
  - Without funding, art cannot survive
(example)

    c. If art loses funding, it will hurt artists, the economy, and America's role as leader in international culture (reason).

        – Great artists would have to emigrate (example)

        – Tourism would suffer; Christo's *The Gates* was controversial but publicly funded and boosted New York economy (example)

  3. Argument Conclusion: Assisting profitable companies and not the arts is hypocritical and would endanger the economy as well as cultural heritage.

C. Third Major Supporting Argument: Much of the greatest art was once controversial and has influenced the course of artistic and scientific evolution.

  1. Transition and Introduction

  2. Reasons and Examples

    a. What was once controversial art has influenced/inspired (reason).

        – Picasso's Cubism, *Guernica* (example)

    b. Controversial art has preserved history and culture for future generations (reason).

        – *Last Supper* still provides clues to the Bible (example)

    c. Controversial art has even helped science (reason).

        – Da Vinci's sketches of human cadavers aided biology (example)

    d. Ceasing funding could potentially jeopardize preserving our history for later generations (reason).
- We know little about the Mayans and Aztecs because art destroyed. What if it were never even made? (example)
- Neglected historical films are gone, lost answers (example)

    e. Ceasing funding could also hamper our knowledge of world history (reason).
- Museums would be forced to close (example)

3. Argument Conclusion: Preventing the creation of art that seems controversial now could not only jeopardize the future of artistic influence but also threaten the preservation of our history for future generations.

III. CONCLUSION
A. Transition to thesis restatement
B. Summary of arguments
C. A new perspective or future idea

Our outline now has a logical flow, with detailed reasoning and examples. It begins with an ethical/emotional appeal by addressing democratic values, then uses logic to reason consistency with existing tradition, and ends by envisioning a sad future without relevant art and a traceable history. While one might be tempted to instead organize the reasons chrono-

logically (beginning with historically controversial art, moving
to consistency in contemporary life, and then discussing the
future of art and democracy), starting with a historical context
would bury the issue and deprive the debate of much needed
urgency.

   Not all of the reasons we'd discussed made it to the
outline. The counterargument that plenty of resources exist
for more traditional forms of art simply didn't fit in logically.
A place for this reason may appear in the writing stage, or it
may simply have to be abandoned—something that frequently
occurs in the transition from thoughts to writing. And remember that each supporting argument is *not* necessarily its own
paragraph—in this case, our arguments will likely stretch out
over several paragraphs when we write our first draft.

Writing the First Draft

When you faced the prospect of writing an essay, you may have expected to simply turn on your computer and start writing—but now you see how many steps are necessary before the writing even begins. Planning and preparation are as important to the writing process as writing the paragraphs that will make up your essay. Without brainstorming, creating arguments, and outlining, you'd be writing your essay blind. You'd get words on the page, no problem—but whether you'll create a coherent, convincing argument is anybody's guess.

Your first draft is the grand finale of the preliminary preparation, where all of your thinking, planning, and outlining come together for the first time. Think that writing the first draft is the hard part? Think again: you've *done* the hard part. Everything you need for your first draft is already at your fingertips, waiting to be put together into essay form. The writing will be much easier now that you've accomplished the beginning stages.

6

Start Early

Students tend to sit down at 6:00 p.m. and say, "Okay. I've got to write my essay tonight." They forget about the distractions they'll encounter: meals, phone calls, a favorite TV show. They find themselves overwhelmed by the pressure to finish, and normal interruptions become major crises. A better strategy is to make a strict but reasonable writing schedule—well before your essay is due.

To make sure you have plenty of time to revise your essay before handing it in, you need to write your first draft at least two days before your paper is due. That way, you'll have a full day to clear your head and come back to your work fresh. Better yet, write a first draft very early, so you can return to it again and again over a period of many days. If this seems extreme, try it once. Your results will be so good that you'll swear by this method for the rest of your writing days.

Ultimate Style

Stay Focused

Try to write in one-hour blocks, with fifteen-minute breaks in between. During the one-hour blocks, force yourself to stay focused: turn off your cell phone, shut your door, and eliminate any other distractions. You don't want to be in the middle of a great thought when something interrupts your concentration. When you reach your scheduled break time, stretch your legs and check your messages, but then get right back to writing.

Remember that thinking is a part of writing. During your one-hour blocks, stay focused but feel free to get up, pace around with your eyes closed, and even talk to yourself. Just because your fingers aren't clacking away at the keyboard doesn't mean you're not writing. Many famous writers are known for their unusual practices to stay focused.

Trust Your Outline

As you write, follow your outline. It shows you the skeleton of your essay—when you write, you add flesh to those bones. You create an essay from your outline by doing five things:

1. Rewriting the thoughts and fragments of your reasons and examples into full sentences
2. Adding material to explain and clarify your points
3. Connecting your ideas together by writing transitions
4. Writing argument introductions and conclusions
5. Writing an introduction and conclusion to your essay

Even with your outline in front of you, don't forget to keep thinking critically. If an idea that looks fine in your outline seems to get garbled when you try to write it out, sit back and think for a moment. More often than not, there's nothing wrong with your outline—you've just forgotten the thinking process that got you to a certain place. Try to retrace your mental steps. Once you remember why you included an idea in your outline, you'll probably be able to connect it to the essay logically.

Not every outline is flawless, of course. There's always a chance that you failed to consider something when you drafted it, and the flaw didn't become apparent to you until you began writing. Don't worry! Just go back to your outline, identify the problem, and correct it in the outline. Then you'll be ready to go again.

Sometimes students throw away their outline at the first sign of trouble and begin writing "without a net." Don't make this mistake; it will undermine all of your careful planning and result in a disorganized paper. Always solve any structural or logic issues in your outline, not on the pages of your essay. You may feel like you're moving backward if you return to your outline, but you're not. You're just firming up your foundation so you can keep on writing well. When you're able to trust your outline, you'll be able to focus on getting your ideas down, not on developing an argument.

Ultimate Style

Remember: It's a Draft

Writing well takes a lot of time and effort, and a great essay has good ideas *and* good writing. But when you're writing a first draft, you should focus first and foremost on the clarity of your argument. Don't get carried away with eloquence, complex sentences, and a stunning vocabulary. You can add style and verve later, when you revise. For your first draft, just make everything as clear as possible. If you slow down too much to check your spelling and doctor your sentences, you'll lose momentum. Keep your mind focused on clearly stating and articulating each and every thought you have. The important thing is to get the first draft written.

Draft the Introduction

The introduction is where you present the topic you're going to discuss and provide your thesis statement. You don't want to say, "In this essay, I will discuss the importance of metal detectors in high schools." This definitely won't draw your readers in. Instead, you should provide a little background information that shows why your topic is important, interesting, or timely.

A good way to describe the overall shape of the introduction is with a simple visual aid: the funnel. Funnels begin with a wide cylindrical opening and then taper quickly to a narrow spout, distilling a large volume of liquid into a much smaller stream:

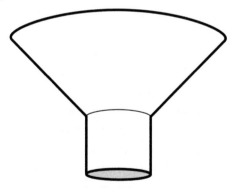

You should structure your introduction in a similar way: start broad, beyond the scope of your essay, and then narrow the subject down until you get to your thesis statement. Remember that you've already written your thesis statement—you should write your introduction around it in order to fill it out and put it in context.

The Beginning   Begin your introduction with a general discussion of your topic. You might provide some background information, a recent controversy related to your topic, or an explanation of why the topic is important to you. Don't begin your introduction *too* broadly. An essay on gun control, for example, would be doomed if the introduction began with the advent of modern weaponry or the invention of gunpowder. You'd need to write countless pages just to reach the issue of gun control. A more reasonable starting point would be a discussion of rising violence rates, an observation on handgun proliferation, or a statistic on crime in America.

After the brief, general discussion of your topic, focus on the specific issue your thesis statement addresses. This strategy grounds readers in your topic, reveals your thought process, and steers them toward your thesis. By writing your introduction this way, you'll gain your readers' confidence and trust with a simple and clear direction of thought. Your thesis statement will seem not just logical but almost inevitable.

A great introduction sets readers up for what they're going to encounter in an essay, and, ideally, it establishes that the writer is knowledgeable, credible, and someone who is going to reveal or argue something skillfully. Your introduction is the first impression you make on your readers.

Introducing Your Arguments   Once you've introduced your topic and included your thesis statement, you will want to include a brief statement that introduces your arguments. Your readers will find out soon enough what your arguments are, but the benefit of telling them up front is that they'll know what to expect going into your essay. You'll seem like a trustworthy, knowledgeable guide.

Length   The introduction should account for approximately 10 percent of your total paper. If you have a five-page paper, this means your introduction should be no more than half a page. You should strive to deliver your introduction in no more than one paragraph. You want to leave ample space for the body of your essay, where you'll have to support your thesis as best you can.

Introduction in Action   Take a look at the draft introduction from our essay on government funding for controversial art. Note that the entire introduction leads up to our thesis statement (underlined below). Since we wrote this first, we wrote the introduction around it, showing why it's important:

> Since the days of Michelangelo, nations have sponsored artists and their work—a tradition that has allowed creativity to flourish and countries to ensure an enduring cultural legacy. In contemporary America, however, this tradition faces imminent danger as the government threatens to cease funding artwork that's considered "controversial." Some see this as a necessary step to put an end to frivolous government spending and ensuring "decency" in public art. Others, meanwhile, assert that this would jeopardize both artistic diversity and American democracy by allowing the government to regulate something that is both inherently subjective and epitomizes our constitutional freedom of expression. <u>Ultimately, a careful analysis of the issue leads to the conclusion that, by ceasing to fund art that some feel is controversial, the government would stifle creative innovation, overstep its boundaries by endorsing</u>

only state-approved art, and set a dangerous precedent for censorship of other artistic mediums, such as film and music.

All the elements needed for an effective introduction are in place: it's about 10 percent of the total length of the essay, it informs the reader of the topic, and it ends with a thesis statement. Furthermore, its structure has the overall shape of a funnel, beginning more broadly and then focusing on the thesis statement.

The first sentence provides a very brief historical example that allows readers to understand the significance of the topic. Then, the very next sentence introduces a contrast ("however") and urgency ("imminent danger") to grab the reader's attention and indicate the purpose for writing the essay. The next two sentences are more focused than the previous ones (remember the funnel!), and describe the basic tenets of the two opposing sides of the issue. This step is not required and can in fact be risky: it may oversimplify the debate. However, including it assures that readers who may be somewhat unfamiliar with the topic to fully appreciate the impact of the very next sentence—the thesis statement.

In our outline (page 69), we planned to discuss controversial art in general, the history of controversial art, and the impending crisis, and, of course, include our thesis statement. All of those elements appear here. When drafting our introduction, we looked at the outline to determine what we planned to include, then fleshed out each idea.

Draft the Body

Since you've spent time thinking carefully about arguments and creating an outline, you already have a good idea of what will go into the body of your essay. In the introduction, you presented your topic and your thesis and (possibly) introduced the arguments you'll use to support it. In the body, you should *explain* the arguments that support your thesis. In other words, this is where you'll build your case.

When you made your outline, you essentially decided how you'll organize the body of your essay. A few things to remember:

- Order your supporting arguments from the most persuasive to the least persuasive.
- Make sure that your reasoning and examples work hand in hand to make your arguments strong and effective.
- Make sure each argument truly does support your thesis, especially if it is a counterargument. Don't be afraid to provide a counterargument that seems to contradict your thesis, as long as you can then shoot it down with your own reasoning and examples.

There's no rule for how much space an argument should take up—it may be one paragraph or several paragraphs. Just be sure to give yourself enough room to present your reasoning and examples and really show how and why that argument supports your thesis. Put yourself in your readers' shoes, and don't let any weaknesses or questions go unacknowledged. If you think

someone could find a reason to disagree with what you're saying, then be sure to address that point thoroughly. Remember,
you're building a case and should cover all your bases.

Topic Sentences and Transitions   Each paragraph in
the body of your essay should start out with a strong topic sentence that lets your readers know that you are moving from one
argument to the next, that you are moving from one aspect of
an argument to another, or that you are presenting a brand-new
idea. The topic sentence should let your readers know exactly
what that paragraph will be about. Topic sentences serve as

transitions that will help your readers follow your logic. They
should function like signs along a highway that alert drivers
to the turns ahead. Often, transitions will look something like
this:

> "Another way in which government censorship of art could
> curtail the creativity of new young artists is . . ."

> "Now that we've shown how censorship of controversial art
> exhibitions can harm the artistic community, let's move on to an
> analysis of how censorship of art sets a dangerous precedent
> for censorship of other artistic mediums . . ."

These brief sentences let you shift gears smoothly and also
underscore that you are in absolute control of your essay,
steering it exactly where you want it to go.

Length   The body of your essay should take up about 75–90 percent of the total length of your essay. Keep in mind that no one argument should eclipse another in size or scale. You don't want to have one argument that takes three pages to detail, followed by another that's only half a page. This imbalance suggests that you either haven't done enough research or that you were writing your essay at the last minute and ran out of time and ideas. Your arguments don't have to be exactly the same length, but they should be somewhat comparable.

In your first draft, however, put this concern out of your mind. You need to focus on getting your ideas down clearly. When you begin to revise, you can look over your work, and if you see vastly different lengths in your arguments, you can add or subtract material as needed.

Draft the Conclusion

The overall shape of the conclusion is familiar: a funnel. This time, however, it's upside down:

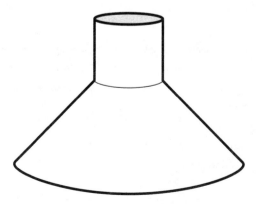

In the conclusion, you should begin narrow—from the thesis and supporting arguments you've just provided—and then widen out to a broader interpretation of the issue you're discussing. Just as you used the introduction to ground your readers in the topic before providing your thesis, you'll use the conclusion to quickly summarize the specifics learned thus far and then hint at the broader implications of your topic, or the future direction in which it will likely grow.

A conclusion is like the end of a movie that will surely have a sequel—it closes the door on one episode but leaves another door open for the next. While you won't be writing a sequel to your essay, you want to show that you've considered your topic beyond the essay's scope. You also want to emphasize yet again how important your topic is, and showing the broader implications of your topic is a way to do this.

Ultimate Style

Tips   There's no patented way to make your conclusion a foolproof success. The right conclusion is only *right* in the context of each individual essay. But here are a few suggestions to inspire you:

- If your essay is on a local or personal issue, provide a logical direction the issue might take if it were on a more universal scale. For example, if you're discussing the importance of making community service a requirement for high school seniors at your school, you could discuss the effects of requiring *all* high school seniors across the country to do community service.

- If your thesis criticizes the status quo of the issue you're discussing, postulate what the future would look like if your solution to the issue were implemented. For example, if your thesis criticizes the absence of affordable, universal health insurance in the United States, you might discuss how establishing a new system of medical coverage would benefit the unemployed.

- For other issue-oriented topics, try taking the "high road"—imagine a future without the quarrelsome debate that has locked the issue in a political stalemate. For example, if you're discussing the right of gay parents to adopt children, you might move the discussion away from sexual orientation and discuss the importance of placing children with loving parents.

- If your essay details an historical event, author, or work of art, try using your conclusion to consider how it would be perceived in modern times, or how our world might be different if the topic in question hadn't existed. For example, in an essay about Orson Welles, you could show how Welles's film work continues to influence filmmakers today.

- Most important, your conclusion must refer back to your topic and thesis. Don't attempt to stuff in unrelated queries or too many abstract thoughts.

Length   Your conclusion should comprise only 5–10 percent of your total essay, so don't attempt to repeat everything you just said. Not only will this be boring, but it's also a waste of space. This is your final chance to prove to readers how important your topic is—and why you're right about your thesis.

Conclusion in Action   In an essay called "Politics and the English Language" by George Orwell, Orwell describes common language errors and shows how they lead to errors in *thinking*. Here's how he concludes his essay:

**Ultimate
Style**

I have not here been considering the literary use of language, but merely language as an instrument for expressing and not for concealing or preventing thought. Stuart Chase and others have come near to claiming that all abstract words are meaningless, and have used this as a pretext for advocating a kind of political quietism. Since you don't know what Fascism is, how can you struggle against Fascism? One need not swallow such absurdities as this, but one ought to recognize that the present political chaos is connected with the decay of language, and that one can probably bring about some improvement by starting at the verbal end. If you simplify your English, you are freed from the worst follies of orthodoxy. You cannot speak any of the necessary dialects, and when you make a stupid remark its stupidity will be obvious, even to yourself. Political language–and with variations this is true of all political parties, from Conservatives to Anarchists–is designed to make lies sound truthful and murder respectable, and to give an appearance of solidity to pure wind. One cannot change this all in a moment, but one can

> at least change one's own habits, and from time to time one can
> even, if one jeers loudly enough, send some worn-out and use-
> less phrase—some *jackboot, Achilles' heel, hot-bed, melting pot,*
> *acid test, veritable inferno* or other lump of verbal refuse—into
> the dustbin where it belongs.

In the first sentence, Orwell reminds us of what he's been discussing in his essay: the relationship between language and thought. In the very next sentence, he acknowledges an absurd argument that represents the illogical extreme to which his own argument may be taken: the idea that "all abstract words are meaningless." In a sense, this is a counterargument: a skeptical reader might very well bring this extreme to Orwell's attention, trying to show him how ridiculous his argument is. Orwell skillfully dismisses that extreme—and avoids potential criticism from readers.

    A refined, more forceful version of his thesis appears halfway through this conclusion: *Political language…is designed to make lies sound truthful and murder respectable….* After making that alarming statement, which he has spent his essay demonstrating, he concludes with a suggested course of action for his readers: if you change your own habits, you may eventually succeed in changing the language itself.

Obey Length Requirements

Essay lengths vary depending on the class, the type of assignment, and your year in school, and you may face a two-page essay, a five-page essay, or anywhere in between or beyond. You might wonder what the leeway is. Just how long *is* a five-page essay? Is 4.75 pages close enough? Is 5.5 pages too long? If your 10,000-word essay is actually 10,047 words, will you be graded down?

A general rule is that your paper should deviate no more than 10 percent from the desired length. If an essay is supposed to be five pages long, and yours is five and a half, you should be fine. If you're assigned a 1,000-word essay, 900 words will likely suffice. There will always be instructors who are true sticklers, and it's always in your best interest to edit your work to reach the desired length, but as long as you're within that 10 percent range, you should be in good shape. When in doubt, always ask your instructor what he or she will accept.

Ultimate Style

First Draft in Action   Below is a sample first draft for our essay on government funding of controversial art. As you read it, pay careful attention to the individual elements we've discussed:

- A brief introduction that provides readers with a context for the topic and a thesis statement
- A transition and introduction for each supporting argument
- A body with a logical flow and interwoven reasons and examples
- Paragraphs with clear topic sentences
- A conclusion that summarizes the thesis without restating it, then explains the significance of the essay in a larger context

Remember that this is a first draft—you'll see errors in grammar, spelling, and punctuation. We'll take care of these when we revise our essay.

We've broken down this draft for you so that you can easily identify each part of the essay.

Andrew Smith
First Draft

INTRODUCTION

Since the days of Michelangelo, nations have sponsored artists and their work—a tradition that has allowed creativity to flourish and countries to ensure an enduring cultural legacy. In contemporary America, however, this tradition faces imminent danger as the government threatens to cease funding artwork that's considered "controversial." Some see this as a necessary step to put an end to frivolous government spending and ensuring "decency" in public art. Others, meanwhile, assert that this would jeopardize both artistic diversity and American democracy by allowing the government to regulate something that is both inherently subjective and epitomizes our constitutional freedom of expression. Ultimately, a careful analysis of the issue leads to the conclusion that, by ceasing to fund art that some feel is controversial, the government would stifle creative innovation, overstep its boundaries by endorsing only state-approved art, and set a dangerous precedent for censorship of other artistic mediums, such as film and music.

BODY: FIRST MAJOR SUPPORTING ARGUMENT

Freedom of expression stands as one of the most cherished rights guaranteed to all Americans. As the First Amendment of the Constitution, it is the corner-stone of our democracy, protecting people's right to free speech, religion, press, and artistic expression. While in Communist China people can be jailed for expressing their ideas, such behavior is not only permitted but also encouraged in America.

When it comes to artistic expression, then, it is clearly not the job of a democratic government to determine what art is "good" or "bad," nor what art is "acceptable" or "unacceptable." By its very nature, art is subjective. What one person sees as "good" art, another may see as "bad." What one person may like, another may dislike. This pertains not only to personal taste, but to style and subject matter as well. The same nude painting can be seen by some as "tasteful" and by others as "obscene," just as some may view an artistic political statement as "relevant" while others view it as "vulgar." In other words, art is a very personal experi-ence for artists and audiences alike, and any attempt by a government to impose classification would be both arbitrary and ineffective.

We should think of other things besides subjectiv-ity. If the government has the right to reject art it feels may be "obscene," what's to stop it from censoring work it feels may be "critical" of its policies? Could the government not suppress art that denounces a political

Ultimate Style

party or attempts to illuminate the truth behind a particularly heinous government policy? While abolishing obscenity may be the intended goal of allowing the government to reject certain art, there's no guarantee that this power would not be abused for political gain.

Censorship knows few bounds, and its application could extend far beyond fine art to include artistic entertainment such as TV, music, and film. Many consider TV shows such as *The Sopranos* and *The Simpsons* as obscene and crude in their depiction of characters with questionable values. Musical acts as diverse as Eminem, U2, and the Rolling Stones have expressed discontent with government policies. Films frequently challenge politicians and their decisions, both directly (*Fahrenheit 9/11*) and indirectly (*Three Kings*). While none of these particular performers or projects was sponsored by the government, they are still subject to federal standards, such as the FCC's. Thus, to grant the government permission to restrict some art sets a dangerous precedent, and it could only be a matter of time before other artistic mediums, as well as our own democracy, are the next to go under the knife.

BODY: SECOND MAJOR SUPPORTING ARGUMENT

Some who oppose the government funding potentially controversial art are not concerned with the content of art as much as the price to taxpayers. They argue that government spending is already too high, and it's unfair for every American taxpayer to pay for something so few actually enjoy. Although this argument may seem justified at first, it does not hold up under scrutiny. While it may be true that not all Americans go to museums and galleries to see the art their taxes support, this is hardly unique to art, as a survey of other taxpayer-supported programs quickly reveals. Public education is supported wholly by taxpayer dollars, and only those under the age of eighteen actually attend school. The construction of professional sports stadiums and arenas is often financed by tax money, despite the fact that not all taxpayers enjoy sports. Taxes fund law enforcement and fire departments, yet few complain that because they haven't been robbed or on fire, their hard-earned tax dollars have been wasted. The fact is simple: government funding of art is consistent with countless other tax-supported programs, and those who are discontent with the system should not single out art as the sole culprit.

If art is not alone in benefiting from federal funding, it is also the recipient of a mere fraction of the money other, more profitable entities collect annually. It's understandable that the construction of bridges and highways requires enormous financial resources; these projects are large, expensive, and do not generate profits. However, few consider that major corporations with billion-dollar profits such as Wal Mart, 3M, and Halliburton receive huge tax subsidies from the government every year. To give billions to America's most profitable companies while denying the NEA its relatively small $100 million budget is nonsensical. Under this model, the average American's tax burden would remain virtually unchanged, but the taxes they pay would go directly to the profitable companies they work for, rather than to artists who need the money to survive. Without support, many artists would turn to low-wage jobs, thus completing a cycle in which the rich get richer, the artists get poorer, and the poor simply get larger in population.

As the above reasoning suggests, artists have much to lose if government support of the arts is ceased. But what about the welfare of America as a whole? Considering how little private support the arts receive, it is likely that many artists with yet unrealized potential would be forced to end their careers. While this may at first sound far from a national crisis, it's important to consider the impact of such an action. By depriving artists of their welfare, the unemployment rate would rise. Even those artists able to find nonart-related jobs would cease to produce art, causing galleries and museums to close or lose revenue. Since these establishments create tax revenue, the overall economy of America would be adversely affected.

In addition to compromising America's economy, repealing funding for the arts would compromise America's role as an international cultural leader. For decades, America has been seen as a major influential force in art, culture, and fashion. This status has led to an international awareness and appreciation of all things American, which in turn attracts tourism, stimulates the economy, and encourages the international community to look to America for innovation and influence. An example of the power of such status can be found in the recent exhibit in New York's Central Park of Christo's installation, *The Gates*. For years, the renowned artist sought to decorate the sidewalks of Central Park with festive gates lined with orange fabric. When New York Mayor Mike Bloomberg finally agreed to fund the costly project with city money, controversy surrounding the work intensified. However, the installation attracted thousands of tourists from around the globe, generated $250 million for the city, and helped New York to maintain its status as a major center of culture.

BODY: THIRD MAJOR SUPPORTING ARGUMENT

A final argument in favor of continued government support of the arts concerns the subjective nature not just of art, but of the term "controversial" as well. It's imperative to note the true meaning of the word *controversial*. *Controversial* does not mean "indecent" or "obscene." *Controversial* means "something that provokes disagreement." While disagreements can be contentious, they are an unavoidable aspect of daily life. For a government to try to stop them would be both overzealous and impossible. In fact, a closer analysis of historical controversies, especially in the arts, shows that controversy can be greatly positive, leading to great advances and innovation in the arts and sciences.

Pablo Picasso is widely considered to be the most influential artist of the last century, and his work has left an indelible mark on the evolution of art. It's important to consider, then, that his work was once considered very controversial. His painting *Guernica* was particularly controversial both stylistically (cubism) and politically (as a harsh depiction of the Spanish Civil War). Yet this controversy proved to be beneficial—the work not only influenced other artists but drew attention to a brutal war led by the Spanish fascist Francisco Franco.

As Picasso's work proves, controversy can have a positive effect of art and society. The work of Leonardo da Vinci, meanwhile, shows controversial art can also further historical awareness and aid scientific advances. Da Vinci's painting *The Last Supper* has endured much controversy throughout the ages, but continues to aid historians and religious scholars in understanding Christianity. Da Vinci also used human cadavers to make numerous anatomical sketches—a very controversial practice that resulted in a better understanding of the biology of the human body.

Considering the proven benefit of controversial art, the potential harm of "protecting" people from it becomes all too clear. If any art deemed controversial were to be censored, we would jeopardize possible scientific advances, hinder cultural awareness, and cease to preserve portrayals of contemporary society for future generations. Ancient cultures such as the Mayans remain a mystery to historians and anthropologists today because so much of their art was destroyed.

Imagine how much less would be known of these cultures had the little art that survived not been made at all? To allow this same fate to befall America would be a tragedy for future generations, both in documenting our history and learning from our mistakes.

CONCLUSION

In summary, it should now be clear that America prospers greatly from providing government support to the arts, despite work that may be considered "controversial." In addition to fostering the arts, this decades-old tradition benefits the economy and assures America is a major international cultural force. Because art and what constitutes "controversial" are both subjective, they defy government classification, and to cease government support would jeopardize freedom of expression, democracy, and the cultural heritage of America now and for years to come. Perhaps if some of the great artists of history such as Michelangelo, Van Gogh, and Picasso were alive and working today, people would view government support of the arts differently. In this sense, it is more crucial than ever to foster the arts in every way possible—doing so will increase the likelihood that an unknown but great artist will be recognized, thrive, and thus provide America with a modern cultural legend.

Commentary Let's briefly examine this first draft. We discussed the introduction on page 79, and here you can see how it

Ultimate Style

does indeed set readers up for what comes next in the essay. The body of the essay is divided into three major supporting arguments, all of which were thoroughly outlined beforehand. Each argument begins with a brief introduction, and transitions indicate the beginning of new thoughts and reasoning. Occasionally, a transition manages to conclude one thought and begin a new one in the same sentence, such as: "Considering the proven benefit of controversial art, the potential harm of 'protecting' people from it becomes all too clear."

Our conclusion fits our requirements as well: the first three sentences of the conclusion are the narrow end of the funnel, where information found within the essay is gathered and summarized. The final part of our conclusion shows how our topic is significant in a larger context.

You may notice some errors or weaknesses in this draft. For example, even though we've followed our outline closely, the organization of the arguments could be stronger, and some of the information seems unnecessary or out of place. The conclusion is too focused on summary; the goal, you may remember, is to demonstrate how the arguments have succeeded in proving your thesis. The last two sentences of the conclusion are intended to be the wider end of the funnel, where the purpose of the essay gains new significance in light of a larger context in which it can be viewed, but here it introduces a new, specific argument rather than broadening the scope of the essay. Now isn't the time to worry about these or other errors—identifying and solving problems with your essay shouldn't be done while you write, but later on in a separate revision process.

Revising Your Work

This rule is a must for all writers: write in drafts, and revise, revise, revise! Ernest Hemingway provides us with perhaps the best (though not the most eloquent) statement on drafts: "The first draft of anything is sh*t." According to him, the purpose of the first draft is to get all of one's thoughts recorded on paper. After that, the editing and rewriting begins, which is where the work truly takes shape.

So just what is revising? Revising involves making large changes, such as reorganizing arguments or revamping your introduction, as well as smaller (yet still very important) changes, such as cleaning up your grammar, rewriting sentences for sophistication and style, and creating the appropriate tone for your work. You've written down your ideas—and revising is how you make them shine.

Take a Day Off

Think of the last argument you had with someone. Later, you undoubtedly replayed the argument in your mind, recalling your words. You probably had a "Eureka!" moment as you thought of a great comeback or witty retort that eluded you earlier. If only you had said *that*! But the argument is over; you lost your chance.

As a writer, you get a second chance to say the right thing. You even get a third chance. You're unlikely to come up with your best lines the first time around, and you should take some time away from your work before you start revising it. Within a few hours of writing, your work is still fresh in your mind, and you won't have the perspective required to see possible changes and improvements. So before revising, take a day off, and don't look at your essay. When you look at it again later, you'll be sure to see errors, as well as new and better ways to state things, that you wouldn't have noticed the first time around.

Revise from the Outside In

The first rule for revision is to revise from the outside in. What does this mean? It means start in broad strokes, targeting the largest and most sweeping problems first. You might address any or all of the following aspects of your essay:

- Organization of thoughts and arrangement of body paragraphs
- Weak or illogical arguments
- Ideas in the introduction and conclusion

You'll probably do a lot of deleting and rewriting during this stage. Once your essay is down on paper, problems in organization and the strength or weakness of your ideas will really stand out.

Only when this large-scale work is complete should you focus on smaller issues, including:

- Sentence structure
- Word choice
- Proofreading (grammar, misspellings, and punctuation)

When you revise from the outside in, you won't waste time looking up a word that you may very well delete later, or struggling with the specific phrasing of a sentence that you're going to change anyway. Think of the final step, proofreading, as the final costume adjustment before you go on stage.

Revisit the Body

When you revise, you'll probably find yourself focusing on the body of your essay more than any other part. The introduction and conclusion are both shorter and to the point, while the body takes up the bulk of your essay and is where your argument truly comes alive. The body needs to be handled carefully so that you can create the most convincing argument possible. You should focus on reorganizing the body for logic and effectiveness, then check to make sure you haven't created problems while trying to solve them.

Reorganizing   The body relies on very detailed, logical progressions and connections. When you outline, you make your best effort to arrange your reasoning and examples logically. But when you start writing, those steps sometimes get shifted around, and better ways of organizing often present themselves *after* you've written your first draft. Revision is the time to reorganize. If a section seems out of place, move it around until you find a better spot for it. You may also decide to delete material that no longer works effectively.

Keep in mind that reorganizing creates a ripple effect: if you change one thing, you may have to change something else. For example, a particular argument may rely on an earlier argument in order to make sense, and if you move that earlier argument, then you'll have to move the other argument as well. Pay attention to the overall logic of your essay so that you don't inadvertently *create* problems when you're trying to solve them.

Looking over our essay, we managed to find one section in particular that seems out of place, logically speaking. Take a look at the essence of each of our three arguments:

Ultimate Style

First argument: The nature of art and controversy
If a government supports some art while rejecting other art, it is in essence practicing censorship–the bane of a democratic system.

Second argument: The notion of public funding
Arts funding is not only consistent with other forms of public funding, but its dissolution would jeopardize the future of American art.

Third argument: The nature of art and controversy
Much of the greatest art was once controversial and has influenced the course of artistic and scientific evolution.

You can see that two very similar arguments—the first and third—are separated by an unrelated argument, when it would make more sense for similar arguments to appear together in the essay. While the order of arguments seemed logical when we were outlining, it becomes awkward in the actual first draft. By jumping back and forth like this, the overall logic of the essay is compromised. The arguments themselves are fine—but the order in which we present them needs improvement.

In our revision, we'll switch the second and third arguments so that we move logically from one aspect of the issue to the next. We'll explore all aspects of the nature of art and controversy before moving on to the idea of public funding.

Checking Setups and Payoffs   The terms "setup" and "payoff" come from the field of drama. A setup is a detail placed early on in a story that helps to explain something (pays off) later on. For example, in the film *Aliens*, we discover in the first half-hour that Ripley has been trained to use large, robotic power-loaders (manned forklifts). This setup has its payoff at the end of the film, when Ripley uses a power-loader to kill the Queen Alien. The setup is necessary: without it, it would seem far too convenient that Ripley knew how to use such a complex machine just when she needed it at the end.

In an essay, setups and payoffs occur when you inform your readers in an earlier section that you'll touch on something later on. Usually, setups appear in the introduction, when you describe the arguments you'll use to support your thesis. The problem that sometimes occurs during revision is that you inadvertently move or delete one of the payoffs. If this happens, you end up saying you're going to do something that you don't actually do. You could wind up misleading your readers.

After reorganizing your thoughts, you should immediately verify your setups and payoffs. Check to see if you've moved or deleted any of them. If you did, you should revise the rest of the essay to reflect that change. If you delete a setup, you should delete the related payoff. If you delete a payoff, you should delete the related setup.

Checking Setups and Payoffs in Action Now that we've reorganized the arguments in our essay, we should look it over to make sure we don't have any missing setups or payoffs. After a little reading, we discover that the first line of the new second argument is illogically set up:

**Ultimate
Style**

> A final argument in favor of continued government support of the arts concerns the subjective nature not just of art but of the term "controversial" as well.

This *used to be* our third and final argument, but now it's our second argument, so we need to change the transition so that it doesn't say "final." Otherwise, readers will be puzzled when they discover there is actually one more "final" argument. We could simply change the word "final" to "second," but perhaps there's a better way to revise the transition now that there's more of a logical flow from the first to the second argument:

> Just as an analysis of art shows that it is inherently subjective and thus defies classification, an analysis of the term "controversial" reveals that its negative connotation is unwarranted.

Here, we've clearly linked two related arguments, and readers will understand what we're about to discuss, and why.

An example of a missing setup can be found in the new second argument, which mentions the National Endowment for the Arts (NEA). This organization is the key target of proposed government budget cuts, and to first mention it this far into the essay is inappropriate. It seems to come out of nowhere because it isn't identified earlier on in a setup. Therefore, a setup of the NEA should be added to the introduction:

> In contemporary America, however, this tradition faces imminent danger as the government threatens to cease funding to organizations such as the National Endowment for the Arts (NEA) that provide grants to artwork that some consider "controversial."

Check Topic Sentences

Every paragraph in your essay should begin with a strong, clear topic sentence that tells readers exactly what your paragraph will be about. Readers shouldn't have to guess what's going on in your essay—it's up to you to lead them through it. You can think of a topic sentence as the thesis of the paragraph. It explains what the paragraph is about and places it within the context of your argument.

When you're revising, look at each topic sentence and make sure it's clear. If you don't understand what the paragraph will be about just by reading the topic sentence, revise the sentence. Take a look at this example:

WEAK: We should think of other things besides the subjectivity
of art.

STRONG: As if the subjectivity of art being at stake were not
enough, there's also the grave consideration of censorship.

The weak topic sentence doesn't tell us much about what the
paragraph will be about. What *things*? Why should we think
about them? The revision gives us specific information: besides
subjectivity, we should also think about censorship. We know
exactly what the paragraph will be about.

**Ultimate
Style**

Critique Your Arguments

When you're planning your essay, arguments sometimes seem
strong and convincing—then fall apart once you actually
include them in your essay. During the revision process, look
carefully at your arguments and ask yourself the following
questions:

- Are my reasons appropriate to my audience?
- Are my reasons supported by good examples?
- Does the argument leave any room for doubt?
- Is this argument *vital* to the logic and power of my essay? In
  other words, would the essay be weaker if I took it out?
- Does the argument make a unique, well-conceived point
  that supports the thesis?
- Is there a stronger argument that I've overlooked?

Every argument you include should be convincing and well-conceived, with good reasons and examples, and it should take into account any counterarguments your readers might have. It should also be absolutely vital to your essay. Removing an argument should have a significant and negative impact—if this isn't the case, the argument probably isn't strong or important enough to keep. Consider deleting it and replacing it with a better argument—or just deleting the argument altogether. Sometimes, it's okay to eliminate an argument entirely if the rest of your arguments are strong enough on their own.

Revising Arguments in Action In our essay on government funding for controversial art, one argument in particular lacks sufficient logic and persuasive power. It is the very first argument concerning the subjective nature of art:

> When it comes to artistic expression, then, it is clearly not the job of a democratic government to determine what art is "good" or "bad," nor what art is "acceptable" or "unacceptable." By its very nature, art is subjective. What one person sees as "good" art, another may see as "bad." What one person may like, another may dislike. This pertains not only to personal taste but to style and subject matter as well. The same nude painting can be seen by some as "tasteful" and by others as "obscene," just as some may view an artistic political statement as "relevant" while others view it as "vulgar." In other words, art is a very personal experience for artists and audiences alike, and any attempt by a government to impose classification would be both arbitrary and ineffective.

While this argument successfully demonstrates the subjective nature of art, there's insufficient logic to reason that this would make the government's attempts to label art *wrong*. Furthermore, although this paragraph is focused on art's subjectivity, the introduction that precedes it is focused on democracy. In essence, the problem is that two distinct thoughts have been crammed into one paragraph. The first thought is that art's subjectivity makes labeling *unachievable*. The second thought is that freedom of expression makes labeling *unethical*. By combining these two thoughts, the message lacks conviction and clarity. The argument and introduction should be revised to develop two related but distinct thoughts with a logical progression as follows:

Ultimate Style

> To fully understand the role between government and controversial artwork, it is first necessary to analyze the distinct nature of art. Art, by definition, is subjective. What one person likes, another may dislike. What one person sees as "good" art, another may see as "bad." This pertains not only to personal taste but to style and subject matter as well. Some may feel a nude painting is "tasteful" while others find it "obscene," just as artistic political statement can be viewed as "relevant" by one person and "vulgar" by another. In other words, art is a very personal experience for artists and audiences alike, and a consensus about the quality, value, or acceptability of art would be impossible to reach. How, then, can a government determine whether a work of art is categorically "obscene" or "tasteful," "relevant" or "vulgar," or any other quality? Quite simply, it cannot, and therefore should not attempt to. Personal taste and artistic value are simply not qualities a government can, nor should, legislate.

In addition to being subjective, art is also an act of expression. Because of this, it is protected by the First Amendment of the Constitution, one of the most cherished rights guaranteed to all Americans. While in Communist China people can be jailed for expressing their ideas, such behavior is not only permitted but encouraged in a democracy like America. For a government to begin deciding for its citizens what art is and isn't acceptable, it would be greatly overstepping its bounds. In essence, this practice results in the abolishment of all but state-approved art, a concept that threatens the very fabric of democracy.

Critique Your Introduction

After you've revised the body of your essay, you can tackle the introduction. Creating an effective introduction can be one of the most difficult parts of the writing process, and once you've drafted the essay, you may change your mind about how your introduction is working. You may be able to see new possibilities, or you might see a better angle from which to approach your thesis. During the revision process, ask yourself the following questions:

- Does your introduction start too broadly? Make sure you haven't started so far beyond the scope of your topic that the introduction is almost unrelated.
- Is the background material relevant? Your introduction should provide material that will help readers understand the importance or purpose of your essay.
- Is the introduction interesting? Remember: this is your readers' first impression of your essay. Draw them in.
- Is your thesis presented clearly, and does it arise naturally from the discussion you've presented? Don't let your thesis feel "tacked on."

Ultimate Style

- Is the introduction authoritative? Make sure you don't sound uncertain or wishy-washy—you want your readers to see you're a credible source of information.

You may change just a few sentences, or you may rewrite the introduction entirely. Do whatever you need to do to create a compelling introduction to your thesis—and to establish yourself as a writer your readers should listen to.

Revising the Introduction in Action   Our introduction provides a very brief history, a sense of urgency and purpose, and, now that we've added the setup of the NEA (see page 107), appropriate focus—as well as, of course, a thesis statement (underlined):

> Since the days of Michelangelo, nations have sponsored artists and their work—a tradition that has allowed creativity to flourish and countries to ensure an enduring cultural legacy.

In contemporary America, however, this tradition faces imminent danger as the government threatens to cease funding to organizations such as the National Endowment for the Arts (NEA) that provide grants to artwork that some consider "controversial." Some see this as a necessary step to put an end to frivolous government spending and ensuring "decency" in public art. Others, meanwhile, assert that this would jeopardize both artistic diversity and American democracy by allowing the government to regulate something that is both inherently subjective and epitomizes our constitutional freedom of expression. <u>Ultimately, a careful analysis of the issue leads to the conclusion that, by ceasing to fund art that some feel is controversial, the government would stifle creative innovation, overstep its boundaries by endorsing only state-approved art, and set a dangerous precedent for censorship of other artistic mediums, such as film and music.</u>

However, there are still problems. First, the discussion leading up to the thesis is so evenhanded and balanced that our thesis statement seems tacked-on and arbitrary. If you wanted to include a thesis statement with the opposite opinion, you wouldn't have to change the introduction very much. While evenhandedness can be a strength, it's important to gradually hone in on a thesis statement so that readers clearly understand the direction your introduction is taking.

The second problem is the thesis statement itself, which focuses too much on listing arguments that will be presented in the body and not enough time stating a strong and irrevocable opinion. Introducing arguments can be a good way to prepare your reader for the essay, but this should not reduce your thesis statement to a mere preview of things to come. The thesis also suffers in light of the sentences immediately preceding it, which state specific views on the issue. The views are so specific, in fact, that they make our thesis seem like a copycat opinion—one that just regurgitates what others have said.

Take a look at how we revise our introduction, and, ultimately, our thesis statement (underlined below):

> Since the days of Michelangelo, nations have sponsored artists and their work—a tradition that has allowed creativity to flourish and countries to ensure an enduring cultural legacy. In contemporary America, however, this tradition faces imminent danger. Because some consider work by artists who receive federal grants to be "controversial," the government is now threatening to cut funding to organizations such as the National Endowment for the Arts (NEA). While some contend that this measure would put an end to frivolous government spending and ensure "decency" in public art, these arguments fail to consider the impact upon artistic innovation and diversity, as well as the threat to our constitutional freedom of expression. <u>As a careful analysis will reveal, it is not the government's job to determine the value of art, and to cease funding work that some feel is controversial would undermine democracy, adversely affect the economy, and set a dangerous precedent for censorship of other artistic mediums.</u>

Here, we've made the introduction less evenhanded—even before we get to the thesis statement, readers will have a clear understanding of our opinion on the subject. We present the opposing side—the people who value "decency" in public art—then explain why this side is faulty. Our introduction then delivers a clear and undeniable opinion in our thesis statement.

Critique Your Conclusion

Since your conclusion should be inextricably connected to the rest of your essay, you should revise it last. If you've made a lot of changes to your essay, chances are that you'll have to take a heavy hand when you revise your conclusion. Your conclusion should gather all of your main points together, then sweep them up into a larger statement about your topic. When revising your conclusion, ask yourself these questions:

- Have you summarized your arguments succinctly? Remember: your conclusion needs to be more than just a summary, so don't spend too much time rehashing old material.
- Have you explained how your arguments have proven your thesis?
- Have you broadened your topic to show its relevance or importance beyond the scope of your essay?
- Is the conclusion a vital, connected part of your essay? It shouldn't feel "tacked on." If you chop off the conclusion, your essay should be weaker.

The conclusion is often the most difficult part of an essay to get right, and you may have to work through a few drafts before you manage to create one that ties your essay together effectively.

The good news is that everything you need to revise your conclusion is right in front of you, in the body of your essay. The trick is to synthesize your ideas and show how they relate to both your thesis and the world beyond your essay.

Revising the Conclusion in Action   Take a look at our conclusion from the first draft of our essay:

> In summary, it should now be clear that America prospers greatly from providing government support to the arts, despite work that may be considered "controversial." In addition to fostering the arts, this decades-old tradition benefits the economy and assures America is a major international cultural force. Because art and what constitutes "controversial" are both subjective, they defy government classification, and to cease government support would jeopardize freedom of expression, democracy, and the cultural heritage of America now and for years to come. Perhaps if some of the great artists of history such as Michelangelo, Van Gogh, and Picasso were alive and working today, people would view government support of the arts differently. In this sense, it is more crucial than ever to foster the arts in every way possible–doing so will increase the likelihood that an unknown but great artist will be recognized, thrive, and thus provide America with a modern cultural legend.

Our draft conclusion has numerous problems. It's too focused on summary, and it doesn't provide a larger context in which our essay gains greater significance. The first sentence is essentially a throwaway: it simply rewords the thesis without providing new information. It also begins with the phrase

"In summary," which is the equivalent of saying, "Hey, here's my conclusion." This sentence and the two that follow should be revised to show how the arguments have supported the thesis.

The wider end of the funnel—the last two sentences—introduces a new argument instead of providing a new context. It's true that arts funding could give rise to a number of great, modern artists, but the place for an argument like this would be in the body of the essay. Positioned in the conclusion, it feels as though we tried to squeeze a last argument in because we couldn't find a place for it earlier. Instead of forcing in a final argument, we should try to think of the broader implications of the issue. Since freedom of expression has been mentioned in the essay and has far-reaching implications, perhaps expanding on this aspect of the issue will give the conclusion the broader significance it requires.

After revising, our conclusion now looks like this:

By analyzing the cultural, historical, and economic benefits of government support for the arts, as well as the personal nature of both art and what constitutes "controversy," it becomes clear that America prospers greatly from this time-honored tradition. To cease government support would provide very little relief to taxpayers, but it would greatly jeopardize democracy, the economy, and the cultural heritage of America now and for years to come. Ultimately, those who express anger at the notion that potentially "offensive" art can be found in America should consider that, in expressing their opinion, they are utilizing the same constitutional freedom of expression that they wish to abolish for others. Perhaps it is not until all freedom of expression is rescinded that those who claim to love democracy will realize how much they miss it.

Restructure Sentences

To ensure that your essay flows well and has a certain level of sophistication, you should scrutinize your sentence structure and make sure it has maximum effectiveness. The most important rule is to vary your sentence structure. Sentences that have the same shape and length are tedious. Because clarity is the goal when writing a first draft—rather than sophistication and efficiency—your sentences may be a little bland the first time around. In the revision process, you get the chance to rework the structure of your sentences so they sparkle.

As an example of boring, unsophisticated sentence structure, take a look at the following paragraph:

> Sentence structure is very important. Sentence structure is part of what makes your essay exciting. Sentence structure, if it is monotonous and unchanging, can make your essay sound boring and unsophisticated. Sentence structure is important in all kinds of essays. Sentence structure is an important element to include in the revision process.

The sentence structure is very basic. Most of the sentences are roughly the same length, they all start with the same words, and they all have the same basic structure. You can revise similar problems in your own work by doing four things:

1. Varying sentence length
2. Varying sentence beginnings
3. Using effective phrasing
4. Avoiding repetition

Varying Sentence Length   The length of a sentence can have a huge impact on how it sounds. Many people assume that long, complex sentences sound more sophisticated, but this simply isn't true. The best writers use lengthy, complex sentences only when absolutely necessary, such as in these two instances:

1. When the sentence includes a list that can't be broken up: *Virginia Woolf wrote many novels during her lifetime, including* Mrs. Dalloway, To the Lighthouse, The Waves, The Years, A Room of One's Own, *and* Orlando.

2. When the concept being discussed is inherently "wordy" (such as chemical compounds, intricate technical or scientific subjects, or lengthy proper names): *When half of the acid molecules in an aqueous solution are ionized, [A-] = [HA]; as a result, $Ka = [H3O+]$, and taking the negative logarithm of both sides of this equation gives $pKa = pH$ when [A-] = [HA].*

Otherwise, the best writers aim for clarity, which comes in varying lengths and sizes. Keep these ideas in mind:

- Extremely short sentences grab the reader's attention: *He suddenly died.*
- Extremely long sentences confuse the reader, unless they contain lists or cumbersome names and titles:

   Before making any decisions about whether governments should or should not fund art that may be viewed by many people as "obscene," a careful examination, performed by many people and over a significant period of time, not simply a month or even the length of one exhibition, must be performed, documented, published, and analyzed with an eye toward long-term consequences.

Varying Sentence Beginnings   Take a look at these drab and repetitive sentences:

Sentence structure is very important. Sentence structure is part of what makes your essay exciting.

Ultimate Style

They both start with the same noun + verb combination ("sentence structure is"), so there's no flow to them. They're also inefficient and should be combined into one sentence:

Sentence structure is very important, and it's part of what makes your essay exciting.

As you reread your work, make sure no two sentences fall prey to such repetitive structure. If they do, rewrite them.

There is an exception to this rule: at times, you might choose to use a repetitive structure to make a point. But if that's not your goal, aim for sentences with more natural dynamics.

Using Effective Phrasing   There are a few simple "magic words" that you can use to keep your writing engaging:

• *Additionally, Also,* and *Furthermore* create momentum. They indicate that the next sentence follows directly from the previous one, and keep your sentences moving forward.

For example:

> Furthermore, *sophisticated sentence structure increases your credibility as a writer.*

- Words and phrases such as *Therefore, Due to this, Thus,* and *With this in mind* establish a cause-and-effect relationship, logically linking your thoughts. This helps brew expectation in your readers' minds. For example:

> With this in mind, *we can understand why good writing in general is vital to creating an essay that is convincing and memorable.*

- Use *However, Although,* and *Despite* to create an immediate sense of contrast and conflict. People are naturally drawn to conflict, and these words will draw your readers in, creating anticipation. For example:

> Although *many students believe that good writing can mask weak ideas, even the best writing will not lead to a good grade if the essay does not present a well-supported argument.*

You may think that assigning so much meaning to these simple words is hyperbole, but it's not. Like signposts on a road, these words signal the direction of your sentences, trigger anticipation, and stress that you, the writer, are in control.

Avoiding Repetition   Repetitive writing sounds unsophisticated and sloppy, and the perfect time to address this problem is during the revision process. Repetition can occur in two different ways:

- The same word, phrase, or clause is used over and over again in an essay. Sometimes it will be something small and trivial (a word repeated twice in one sentence), but often it will be a more overriding problem (such as a distinct phrase that's used too frequently, such as *In the end,* or *Furthermore*):

    Attempts to censor controversial *art often create a great deal of* controversy *in the art community.*

    To solve this problem, you can try substituting a synonym for the offending word:

    Attempts to censor controversial *art often create* anger *and* debate *in the art community.*

- The sentence structure itself is repetitive, even if the words in the sentences are different. You might have a lot of very simple, declarative sentences, which can make your work sound choppy:
  Structure is important in writing. Sentences should be of different lengths. Essays with similar sentence structure are dull.

To solve this problem, you'll have to rewrite the sentence or sentences. Here, we combined these three choppy sentences to create one sophisticated sentence:

Structure is important in writing, and sentences with similar structure, such as those that do not vary in length, result in dull essays.

Revising Sentence Structure in Action   As an example of poor sentence structure, let's look at the following paragraph from our essay:

> Just as an analysis of art shows that it is inherently subjective and thus defies classification, an analysis of the term "controversial" reveals that its negative connotation is unwarranted. It's imperative to note the true meaning of the word *controversial*. "*Controversial*" does not mean "indecent" or "obscene." *Controversial* means "something that provokes disagreement." While disagreements can be contentious, they are an unavoidable aspect of daily life. For a government to try to stop them would be both overzealous and impossible. In fact, a closer analysis of historical controversies, especially in the arts, shows that controversy can be greatly positive, leading to great advances and innovation in the arts and sciences.

This paragraph is fine for a first draft, but the sentence structure is very basic. Though the first and last sentences have an appropriate length and a natural flow, most of the sentences are roughly the same length, which creates a choppy effect.

Two sentences in a row begin with the same word—*contro-versial*—and that word is overused to the point of becoming repetitive and annoying. By applying the tools explained in this chapter, we can revise our paragraph:

> Just as an analysis of art shows that it is inherently subjective and thus defies classification, an analysis of the term "controversial" reveals that its negative connotation is unwarranted. It's imperative to note that *controversial* does not mean "indecent" or "obscene" but "something that provokes disagreement." While disagreements can be contentious, they are an unavoidable aspect of daily life, and for a government to try to stop them would be both overzealous and impossible. In fact, a closer analysis of historical controversies, especially in the arts, shows that controversy can be greatly positive, leading to great advances and innovation in the arts and sciences.

Now, there is a better balance in terms of sentence lengths, as well as less repetition of the word *controversial*. The addition of the word *rather* creates conflict, and linking related sentences has created cause and effect. The result is a paragraph with a natural flow and a more easily comprehensible thought process behind it.

Write with Conviction

Students who think nothing of brashly declaring "Hands down, *The Simpsons* is the best TV show ever!" often turn into spineless wallflowers when writing essays, including statements such as, "I feel that Mark Rothko's abstract paintings are kind of sublime." Afraid that their opinions might be wrong, students use buffers such as "I feel," "To me," and "I think"—which ultimately water down the conviction of their writing.

You should avoid timid, wishy-washy language at all costs. You won't get a better grade for writing, "I believe Shakespeare was trying to …" instead of "Shakespeare was trying to …"—you may even be graded down for not taking a strong stance. Essays need to be persuasive, and it's tough to persuade your readers of anything when your sentences lack confidence. Conviction sells your ideas and opinions to your readers. By writing with confidence and strength, you exude a natural assurance that people will trust. Good ideas presented in timid and modest ways raise doubts, while good ideas with conviction behind them foster faith.

When you revise, give your writing as much conviction as possible. You should do three things:

1. Write with conviction even if you're not sure something is fact.
2. Avoid the passive voice.
3. Avoid using "I" whenever possible.

Not Quite Fact If you don't feel comfortable stating something as fact, you should still write with conviction. Remember that an essay is, at heart, an *opinion* that you back up with logical arguments. Even if you know there's room for doubt in what you're saying, you can still write with conviction by using one of the following terms:

- Indicates
- Suggests

These options allow you to say, "I believe this, but there's still room for debate."

Ultimate Style

> WEAK: *It seems to me* that the number of abstract paintings Paul Klee produced during the rise of the Nazi regime *probably meant* that he found it difficult to paint what he saw around him.

> STRONG: The number of abstract paintings Paul Klee produced during the rise of the Nazi regime *indicates* that he found it difficult to paint what he saw around him.

The Passive Voice You create the passive voice when you use any form of the verb "to be" plus the past participle of a verb. Some examples of passive voice verbs are: *were given, is loved, was thought.* Passive voice weakens the conviction in your essay because passive verbs either take the emphasis away from the subject or have no clear subject. For example:

> The girl *was loved.* → Who loved her?
>
> Harry *was given* the gift. → Who gave it to him?
>
> Andrew *was considered* by Skip for the job. → Skip is the one doing the considering, but he isn't the subject of the sentence.

Make your sentences strong by using active voice instead of passive. In the following examples, notice how powerful the subject and verb become when the active voice replaces the passive:

> PASSIVE: In 1962, Pete Best *was replaced* by Ringo Starr as the Beatles' drummer.
>
> ACTIVE: In 1962, Ringo Starr *replaced* Pete Best as the Beatles' drummer.

> PASSIVE: You *will be charged* two dollars to use this ATM machine.
>
> ACTIVE: This ATM machine *will charge* you two dollars to use it.

Passive voice isn't always wrong, however, and, at times, it simply sounds better:

> PASSIVE BUT GOOD: France *is known* for its wide selection of fine cheeses.
>
> ACTIVE BUT UGLY: People *know* France for its wide selection of cheeses.

Using "I"   You should find out if your instructor has any rules about using the first-person point of view (I, me, my, mine, etc.) in your essay. Many students believe that using the first-person is always wrong—but this isn't the case. The first-person can be useful in certain types of essays, such as an essay in which you recount a personal story or have firsthand experience with your topic. However, you shouldn't use the first-person automatically—use it deliberately, with a purpose in mind.

Using the first-person draws attention to you as the writer, and this isn't always appropriate. Sometimes this can weaken your argument, since readers may wonder why they should listen to you. The general and imaginary "we" is sometimes more acceptable, but even this can weaken the persuasiveness of your essay.

Ultimate Style

You can almost always find a way to avoid any self-reference. Take a look at these examples:

> WEAK: To further illustrate *my* belief that China's human rights record may be hampering its economic prosperity, *I'll* now focus on the country's role in the United Nations.

> BETTER: To further illustrate how China's human rights record hampers its economic prosperity, *we'll* now focus on the country's role in the United Nations.

> BEST: A further illustration of how China's human rights record hampers its economic prosperity appears in the country's role in the United Nations.

All three examples are saying the same thing, and all three are "correct," but the third example is most authoritative.

Use Familiar Words

Take a look at this sentence, which shows what often happens when student meets thesaurus:

> *Though often repudiated by more obdurate students, composition is most eloquent when pellucid and intelligible; the verbiage intrinsic to exceedingly abstruse phraseology does not impress nor elucidate, but merely obfuscate.*

Students mistakenly believe that if they pack their essays with the most advanced, sophisticated words they can find, they'll sound smart. Instead, they just sound like they have a big thesaurus. The fundamental goal of writing is to convey concepts and ideas through language, and the best writing is clear writing. Clear writing is the choice and combination of words that makes your ideas as comprehensible as possible to your readers. Writing that lacks clarity is difficult to follow and makes your ideas confusing. There are no such things as good and bad words, simple and complex words, or fancy and mundane words; there are only words that help a reader to understand a given concept, and words that hinder that endeavor.

Guidelines   To make your writing crystal clear, consider these three guidelines:

1. **Words from a thesaurus aren't inherently better than words from daily conversation.**

Some unfamiliar words exist to convey a subtle nuance that the familiar words don't. So if you want to say *complicate*, don't change it to *obfuscate* just to sound fancy. Consult your dictionary and make sure *obfuscate* is closer to the true meaning of what you want to say before using it.

2. **Formal language surrounded by natural language looks and sounds out of place.**

   Don't throw in a formal or big word just to make a more pedestrian sentence look smarter. Imagine if you did this in everyday speech:

   Natural: Do you want to go to the dance tonight?
   Unnatural: Do you want to venture to the dance tonight?
   Eighteenth-century Nerd-speak: Would you care to venture to the ball this eve?

   Stilted language doesn't make you sound smart—it makes you sound silly. Keep your language consistent and natural.

3. **Know the meanings of the words you use.**

   You should get to know a new word before you throw it into an essay. The more you understand a word's nuances, the better you'll be able to use it. The fact is that *go* and *venture*, while synonyms, have subtle differences in meaning. Don't just toss words around—think carefully of their specific implications.

Learning New Words   When you're trying to find or learn new words, look beyond your thesaurus. Your thesaurus is useful, but it doesn't provide you with words in context. If you discover a new word in a newspaper or book, however, its context is right there on the page. Look the word up and keep an eye out for it in the future. Start using it in conversations. It will eventually become part of your natural vocabulary, and you'll be able to use it naturally in your writing. This process ensures that you won't sound like just another student with a thesaurus—instead, you'll sound like someone with a naturally rich vocabulary.

Manage Tone

The tone of your essay is very important, as it will determine whether you can effectively connect to your audience. If you choose the wrong tone, you might lose your readers' trust—and even offend them. Tone tends to be subjective, open to interpretation, and difficult to identify. It's a result of expression, intention, and suggestion—all of which are frequently misunderstood.

When we speak, tone is usually present in our voices more than in our choice of words. Just by changing our voices, we can convey that we are polite, annoyed, desperate, or sarcastic. When we write, we have no audible tone of voice. But there's still plenty of tone in the words we choose and how we phrase our ideas:

Polite: Not all controversial art is actually "obscene."

> **Annoyed:** It should be obvious to everyone that not all controversial art is "obscene."
>
> **Sarcastic:** Some conservative critics would label even Degas's work "obscene."

Tone is usually indicative of the response people want from their readers or listeners. Since most people want to impress with their essays, they strive to write with a certain formality, poise, and intelligence. But there are other options as well. Many essays are humorous; others are angry and impassioned. Whatever tone you choose, be sure it's consistent and appropriate.

Consistency   Consistency means maintaining an even tone throughout an essay. If an essay starts off as very earnest and sincere, then suddenly becomes humorous, readers will be thrown off. They'll be distracted from your ideas if they confront confusion and inconsistency in your tone.

If you're going to write something humorous, make sure you establish that tone at the beginning and keep it consistent throughout. You can still inject some thought-provoking ideas into your essay, but your presentation might have to have some levity, such as through satire and irony. Likewise, you should feel free to point out something amusing in an otherwise serious essay, but keep it short and make sure it's appropriate. Make sure you determine your tone before you write. That way, you won't find yourself tempted to switch halfway through.

Appropriateness   Some essays allow for tonal interpretation and might even beg for a humorous take on the issue. A paper on what you did over your summer vacation encourages you to speak with a colloquial tone and use the first-person. An essay on the Holocaust, on the other hand, probably isn't a good time to break out the jokes. You should always consider your audience, topic, and course before choosing a tone that's too adventurous.

Tone in Action   Bill Bryson, a travel writer, is famous for the hilarious, self-deprecating tone of his essays. Take a look at the first two paragraphs from "To the North," an essay in a collection called *Neither Here Nor There* (1992):

> In winter, Hammerfest is a thirty-hour ride by bus from Oslo, though why anyone would want to go there in winter is a question worth considering. It is on the edge of the world, the northernmost town in Europe, as far from London as London is from Tunis, a place of dark and brutal winters, where the sun sinks into the Arctic Ocean in November and does not rise again for ten weeks.
>
> I wanted to see the Northern Lights. Also, I had long harbored a half-formed urge to experience what life was like in such a remote and forbidding place. Sitting at home in England with a glass of whiskey and a book of maps, this had seemed a capital idea. But now as I picked my way through the gray late December slush of Oslo, I was beginning to have my doubts.

Bryson has gotten himself into an unpleasant, uncomfortable situation, and the tone is one of impending hilarity. We get the sense that he is well traveled—he mentions Tunis and assumes readers know where it is—but also that he is prone to making foolish plans. The image of him at home in England, with whiskey and maps, paints him as a somewhat refined intellectual who perhaps doesn't always know what he's getting into. He calls his idea to travel to the North "half-formed," and he willingly ventures to a place he admits is "remote" and "forbidding."

Of course he's having doubts, as he says in the last sentence—he's headed to the Arctic in the middle of December. "Why anyone would want to go [to Hammerfest] in winter is a question worth considering," he says in the first sentence, and the fact that he himself is on his way there shows that Bryson isn't going to cut himself any slack. He definitely isn't remembering his trip with any nostalgia—the tone is the equivalent of Bryson looking at himself from a distance, shaking his head.

Proofread Your Work

"Proofreading" tends to inspire the kind of muffled groans frequently heard after "Want to see photos of my vacation?" or "Your grandmother met someone she thinks you'll really hit it off with." This reputation is hardly deserved. Proofreading may not be fun, but it's the easiest part of revision, because there are only two possibilities: right and wrong.

Proofreading is a separate step in the revision process. You should proofread for three things:

1. Grammar
2. Spelling
3. Punctuation

When you spend a lot of time with a piece of writing, such as when you're working on revising it, you'll be less likely to notice mistakes. You should take a break and proofread your essay with fresh eyes. Even if you stop just long enough to have a meal or chat with a friend between revising and proofreading, you're much more likely to catch your mistakes. Learn about some of the most common grammar errors in Chapter 10: Crash Course in Grammar.

Format Correctly

Just as professional sports referees are always on the lookout for a cheap shot or a foul, instructors are always on the lookout for students who think they can sneak a fast one by them. They watch for cheating and plagiarism, of course, as well as various formatting techniques students use to make their papers appear to be the specified length. You probably know the tricks of the trade:

Use 14-point font, so fewer words are necessary to fill a line

Select a font like Helvetica that takes up more space

Or a font like Arial Narrow that takes up much less space

Or choose wider margins so that the paper appears to be longer than it really is

Or some ridiculous combination of all of the above

Unless your instructor specifically indicates otherwise, all of
your essays should be formatted as follows:

- The essay should be typed on standard 8.5 × 11 inch white
  paper.
- The top and bottom margins should be one inch; the side
  margins should be 1.25 inches.
- The font should be 12 point Times New Roman.
- The lines should be double-spaced.
- The page number should appear in the upper right-hand
  corner of every page, a half-inch from the top of the sheet.
- Each new paragraph should be indented exactly five spaces
  (half an inch).
- Your pages should be fastened together with either a staple
  or paper clip in the upper left-hand corner.

**Ultimate
Style**

Present Your Work

Presentation binders, glossy sheet protectors, and clear-front
report covers can make your paper look fancy and semiprofes-
sional, but in general, these implementations help you very
little. The content is what really counts. A bad paper in a nice
presentation binder won't fare better than a good paper printed
on economy-grade typing paper. If you want to protect your
paper so it doesn't get mangled in transit, these products are
probably worth the money. If you're hoping for a better grade,
you're better off studying a little harder. Whatever you choose,
make sure your instructor has easy access to your work.

Revision in Action   We've now followed all the steps in
this chapter and applied appropriate changes to our essay. Take
a look at the new-and-improved version, in which we've again
labeled the introduction, arguments, and conclusion:

Andrew Smith
English 101

A Matter of Art and Funds

INTRODUCTION

Since the days of Michelangelo, nations have
sponsored artists and their work—a tradition that has
allowed creativity to flourish and countries to ensure
an enduring cultural legacy. In contemporary America,
however, this tradition faces imminent danger. Because
some consider work by artists who receive federal grants
to be "controversial," the government is now threatening
to cut funding to organizations such as the National
Endowment for the Arts (NEA). While some contend that
this measure would put an end to frivolous government
spending and ensure "decency" in public art, these
arguments fail to consider the impact upon artistic
innovation and diversity, as well as the threat to our constitutional freedom of expression. As a careful analysis
will reveal, it is not the government's job to determine
the value of art, and to cease funding work that some feel
is controversial would undermine democracy, adversely
affect the economy, and set a dangerous precedent for
censorship of other artistic mediums.

BODY: FIRST MAJOR SUPPORTING ARGUMENT

To fully understand the connection between the government and controversial artwork, it is first necessary to analyze the distinct nature of art. Art, by definition, is subjective. What one person likes, another may dislike. What one person sees as "good" art, another may see as "bad." This pertains not only to personal taste but to style and subject matter as well. Some may feel a nude painting is "tasteful" while others find it "obscene," just as an artistic political statement can be viewed as "relevant" by one person and "vulgar" by another. In other words, art is a very personal experience for artists and audiences alike, and a consensus about the quality, value, or acceptability of art would be impossible to reach. How then, can a government determine whether a work of art is categorically "obscene" or "tasteful," "relevant" or "vulgar," or any other quality? Quite simply, it cannot, and therefore it should not attempt to. Personal taste and artistic value are simply not qualities a government can, or should, legislate.

In addition to being subjective, art is also an act of expression. Because of this, it is protected by the First Amendment of the Constitution, which guarantees freedom of speech, one of Americans' most cherished rights. While in Communist China people can be jailed for expressing their ideas, such behavior is not only permitted but encouraged in a democracy like America. A government that decides for its citizens what art is and isn't acceptable would be greatly overstepping its bounds. In essence, this practice results in the

Ultimate Style

abolishment of all but state-approved art, a concept that threatens the very fabric of democracy.

As if the loss of constitutional rights were not enough, there's also the grave consideration of censorship. If the government has the right to reject art it feels may be "obscene," what's to stop it from censoring work it feels may be "critical" of its policies? Could the government not suppress art that denounces a political party or attempts to illuminate the truth behind a particularly insidious government policy? While abolishing obscenity may be the intended goal of allowing the government to reject certain art, there's no guarantee that this power would not be abused for political gain.

Censorship knows few bounds, and its application could extend far beyond fine art to include artistic entertainment such as TV, music, and film. Many consider TV shows such as *The Sopranos* and *The Simpsons* as obscene and crude in their depiction of characters with questionable values. Musical acts as diverse as Eminem, U2, and the Rolling Stones have expressed discontent with government policies. Films frequently challenge politicians and their decisions, both directly (*Fahrenheit 9/11*) and indirectly (*Three Kings*). While these particular performers and projects were not sponsored by the government, they are still subject to federal standards, such as the FCC's. Thus, to grant the government permission to restrict some art sets a dangerous precedent, and it could only be a matter of time before other artistic mediums, as well as our own democracy, are the next to go under the knife.

BODY: SECOND MAJOR SUPPORTING ARGUMENT

Just as an analysis of art shows that it is inherently subjective and thus defies classification, an analysis of the term "controversial" reveals that its negative connotation is unwarranted. It's imperative to note that *controversial*" does not mean "indecent" or "obscene" but rather "something that provokes disagreement." While disagreements can be contentious, they are an unavoidable aspect of daily life, and for a government to try to stop them would be both overzealous and impossible. In fact, a closer analysis of historical controversies, especially in the arts, shows that controversy can be greatly positive, leading to great advances and innovation in the arts and sciences.

Pablo Picasso is widely considered to be one of the most influential artists of the last century, and his work has left an indelible mark on the evolution of art. It's important to consider, then, that his work was once considered very controversial. His painting *Guernica* was particularly controversial both stylistically (cubism) and politically (as a harsh depiction of the Spanish Civil War). Yet this controversy proved to be beneficial—the work not only influenced other artists but drew attention to a brutal war led by the Spanish fascist Francisco Franco.

As Picasso's work proves, controversy can have a positive effect on art and society. The work of Leonardo da Vinci, meanwhile, shows controversial art can also further historical awareness and aid scientific advances. Da Vinci's painting *The Last Supper* has endured much controversy throughout the ages but continues to aid historians and religious scholars in understanding Christianity. Da Vinci also used human cadavers to make numerous anatomical sketches—a very controversial practice that resulted in a better understanding of the biology of the human body.

Considering the proven benefit of controversial art, the potential harm of "protecting" people from it becomes all too clear. If any art deemed controversial were to be censored, we would jeopardize possible scientific advances, hinder cultural awareness, and cease to preserve portrayals of contemporary society for future generations. Ancient cultures such as the Mayans remain a mystery to historians and anthropologists today because so much of their art was destroyed. Imagine how much less would be known of these cultures had the little art that survived not been made at all. To allow this same fate to befall America would be a tragedy for future generations, both in documenting our history and learning from our mistakes.

BODY: THIRD MAJOR SUPPORTING ARGUMENT

Some who oppose the government funding potentially controversial art are not concerned with the content of art as much as the price to taxpayers. They argue that government spending is already too high and that it's unfair for every American taxpayer to pay for something so few actually enjoy. Although this argument may seem justified at first, it does not hold up under scrutiny. While it may be true that not all Americans go to museums and galleries to see the art their taxes support, a survey of other taxpayer-supported programs quickly reveals that this is hardly unique to art. Public education is supported wholly by taxpayer dollars, and only those under the age of eighteen actually attend school. The construction of sports stadiums and arenas is often financed by tax money, despite the fact that not all taxpayers enjoy sports. Taxes fund law enforcement and fire departments, yet few complain that because they haven't been robbed or had their property damaged by fire, their hard-earned tax dollars have been wasted. The fact is simple: government funding of art is consistent with countless other tax-supported programs, and those who are not content with the system should not single out art as the sole culprit.

If art is not alone in benefiting from federal funding, it is also the recipient of a mere fraction of the money other, more profitable entities collect annually. It's understandable that the construction of bridges and highways requires enormous financial resources; these projects are large and expensive and do not generate profits. However, few consider that major corporations with billion-dollar profits, such as Wal-Mart, 3M, and Halliburton, receive huge tax subsidies from the government every year. To give billions to America's most profitable companies while denying the NEA its relatively small $100 million budget is nonsensical. Under this model, the average American's tax burden would remain virtually unchanged, but the taxes they pay would go directly to the profitable companies they work for, rather than to artists who need the money to survive. Without support, many artists would turn to low-wage jobs, thus completing a cycle in which the rich get richer, the artists get poorer, and the poor simply grow in number.

As the above reasoning suggests, artists have much to lose if government support of the arts is ceased. But what about the welfare of America as a whole? Considering how little private support the arts receive, it is likely that many artists with yet unrealized potential would be forced to end their careers. While this may at first sound far from a national crisis, it's important to consider the impact of such an action. If artists lose their welfare, the unemployment rate would rise. Even those artists able to find nonart-related jobs would cease to produce art, causing galleries and museums to close or lose revenue. Since these establishments create tax revenue, the overall economy of America would be adversely affected.

In addition to compromising America's economy, repealing funding for the arts would weaken America's role as an international cultural leader. For decades, America has been seen as a major, influential force in art, culture, and fashion. This status has led to an international awareness and appreciation of all things American, which in turn attracts tourism, stimulates the economy, encourages thousands of foreign students to study art in America, and encourages the international community to look to our country for innovation and influence. An example of the power of such status can be found in the recent exhibit in New York's Central Park of Christo's installation, *The Gates*. For years, the renowned artist sought to decorate the sidewalks of Central Park with festive gates lined with orange fabric. When New York Mayor Mike Bloomberg finally agreed to fund the costly project with city money, controversy surrounding the work intensified. However, the installation attracted thousands of tourists from around the globe, generated $250 million for the city, and helped New York to maintain its status as a major center of culture. Even New Yorkers who disliked Christo's *Gates* had something to smile about: despite controversy and mixed reviews, a government-funded work of art defied skeptical critics by stimulating the city's economy and garnering much publicity for a city still grieving the disaster of the 9/11 terrorist bombings.

Ultimate Style

CONCLUSION

By analyzing the cultural, historical, and economic benefits of government support for the arts, as well as the personal nature of both art and what constitutes "controversy," it becomes clear that America prospers greatly from this time-honored tradition. To cease government support would provide very little relief to taxpayers, but it would greatly jeopardize democracy, the economy, and the cultural heritage of America now and for years to come. Ultimately, those who express anger at the notion that potentially "offensive" art can be found in America should consider that, in expressing their opinion, they are utilizing the same constitutional freedom of expression that they wish to abolish for others. Perhaps it is not until all freedom of expression is rescinded that those who claim to love democracy will realize how much they miss it.

Commentary As you can see, the essay now reads much better. The reorganization of the body has created a more logical flow, the thesis statement is more powerful and opinionated, and the restructuring of sentences has created more clear and balanced prose. In addition to changes already discussed in this chapter, we made many other changes as well to address effectiveness, word choice, clarity, grammar, and punctuation.

Improved argument conclusion for resonance
When we reorganized the body of the essay, the second argument became the last, and it needed a little more power and resonance. We added a brief argument conclusion that emphasizes the emotional significance of Christo's *The Gates*:

> *Even New Yorkers who disliked Christo's* Gates *had something to smile about: despite controversy and mixed reviews, a government-funded work of art defied skeptical critics by stimulating the city's economy and garnering much publicity for a city still grieving the disaster of the 9/11 terrorist bombings.*

Improved sentence structure

The first reason in the third supporting argument is solid, but in the first draft, the sentence was clumsy:

> *While it may be true that not all Americans go to museums and galleries to see the art their taxes support, this is hardly unique to art, as a survey of other taxpayer-supported programs quickly reveals.*

After rereading our work, we realized we could make this idea more effective by rearranging the sentence:

Ultimate Style

> *While it may be true that not all Americans go to museums and galleries to see the art their taxes support, a survey of other taxpayer-supported programs quickly reveals that this is hardly unique to art.*

Improved word choice and phrasing

Heinous, near the end of the first supporting argument, seems a bit dramatic:

> *Could the government not suppress art that denounces a political party or attempts to illuminate the truth behind a particularly heinous government policy?*

A more appropriate word is *insidious*:

Could the government not suppress art that denounces a political party or attempts to illuminate the truth behind a particularly insidious government policy?

We found another instance of weak word choice near the beginning of the last argument:

Taxes fund law enforcement and fire departments, yet few complain that because they haven't been robbed or on fire, their hard-earned tax dollars have been wasted.

Do people themselves really get set on fire? In most cases, the fire department helps people save their property from fire. We reworded to say exactly what we mean:

Taxes fund law enforcement and fire departments, yet few complain that because they haven't been robbed or had their property damaged by fire, their hard-earned tax dollars have been wasted.

We found an awkward phrase in the middle of the last supporting argument. A sentence ends as follows:

. . . the rich get richer, the artists get poorer, and the poor simply get larger in population.

The phrase "the poor simply get larger in population" sounds awkward. We changed it to sound better:

> . . . the rich get richer, the artists get poorer, and the poor simply grow in number.

Improved clarity

Near the end of the last argument, we found a sentence in which it is unclear who or what is performing the action:

> *By depriving artists of their welfare, the unemployment rate would rise.*

Who or what is depriving artists of their welfare? It's unclear, and it's not really the point of this sentence. We rewrote it accordingly:

> *If artists lose their welfare, the unemployment rate would rise.*

Eliminated repetition

Toward the end of the last supporting argument, forms of the word *compromise* appear twice in the same sentence:

> In addition to compromising America's economy, repealing funding for the arts would compromise America's role as an international cultural leader.

We changed the second *compromise* to *weaken* in order to cut down on repetition:

In addition to compromising America's economy, repealing fund-ing for the arts would weaken America's role as an international cultural leader.

Corrected grammar

We found an error in parallelism at the beginning of the third argument:

They argue that government spending is already too high, and it's unfair for every American taxpayer to pay for something so few actually enjoy.

Here, people are marking two arguments: that government spending is too high and that the taxpayers face unfairness. Since this sentence is set up as a two-item list, both of these items must be parallel, starting with "that":

They argue that government spending is already too high and that it's unfair for every American taxpayer to pay for some-thing so few actually enjoy.

Corrected punctuation

At the end of the second argument, we found a punctuation error:

Imagine how much less would be known of these cultures had the little art that survived not been made at all?

Though this sentence poses a hypothetical situation, it isn't a question. It should be followed by a period, not a question mark.

We also found an extra comma at the end of the second argument:

> *Da Vinci's painting* The Last Supper *has endured much controversy throughout the ages, but continues to aid historians and religious scholars in understanding Christianity.*

Since the "but" is not followed by a subject, we don't need the comma:

> *Da Vinci's painting* The Last Supper *has endured much controversy throughout the ages but continues to aid historians and religious scholars in understanding Christianity.*

The SAT Essay

As if there weren't already enough hoops to jump through, tests to take, and hairs to yank out of your head to get into college, the good people at the College Board added one more doozy in 2005: the SAT essay. But there's no need to panic. The skills and strategies that go into writing a good essay for class apply to the SAT essay as well. No matter what topic you encounter on the SAT, you'll be able to write a top-notch essay if you know how to outline, structure, and write well. Remember: the SAT essay is like any other essay. If you can write an essay for class, you can write an essay for the SAT.

The biggest difference between the SAT essay and the essays you write for class is that you'll have to write it in twenty-five minutes, and you won't be able to create multiple drafts and revisions. The SAT essay is a first draft, and it involves a much more simplified application of the essay-writing skills you've learned here. One more note: many of the writing guidelines we provide here can be applied to the ACT essay as well.

Know the Basics

To optimize your essay-writing performance, you need to know the basic details of the SAT essay. Familiarize yourself fully so you won't encounter any surprises when you actually take the test:

- The essay is in the Writing Section.

- You'll have twenty-five minutes to complete it.

- You'll be provided with a Response Sheet, which is simply two pages of lined paper. This is all you're allowed to use—supplementary pages are not permitted.

- You're given only one topic. If you write on another topic, your essay will receive a score of 0.

Ultimate Style

- There will be a small blank space directly below the instructions and essay prompt. It's specifically designed as a place for you to "plan" your essay, which is the College Board's generic term for all the prewriting preparations, including brainstorming, choosing a thesis, and outlining.

- You're not graded on penmanship, but handwriting still counts. Regular human beings read your work, and every word should be legible after a quick glance. Readers won't take the time to try to decipher chicken scratch.

- It's different from a regular essay and what you've learned in this book. You'll have less time to write it, and the essay-graders are looking for a strong first draft—not a polished essay.

Know What Matters

We've explained the three primary criteria that determine your essay grade. In order of importance, they were:

1. A persuasive, convincing argument
2. Analytical thought
3. Good writing

The College Board evaluates the SAT essay similarly. Like teachers grading essays for class, they're looking for a great argument—not a parroting of lectures or class materials. The SAT isn't rooted in any particular class: it's a nationwide test that must give equal opportunity to all students, whether they're studying in a tiny school in rural Alabama, attending an expensive private school in New York City, or being home-schooled in Utah. It's unlikely that these students have read the same books, studied the same period in history, or performed the same physics experiments. To avoid giving any student an unfair advantage, all specific class-based knowledge is taken out of the equation. While you're free (and encouraged) to base some of your examples on things you've learned in class, you'll never be expected to quote Shakespeare, rattle off the entire periodic table, or know a specific date in history.

Your score will depend on six basic criteria:

1. Precise use of language
2. Clarity of expression

3. Sustained focus

4. Logical and coherent presentation of ideas

5. Ample development of a point of view

6. Use of clear reasoning and appropriate evidence

1. Precise Use of Language   *Precision* means being accurate and exact. Make sure you're using accurate words—in other words, pay close attention to *usage*. Words must be used in the correct context and must have the correct meaning. Now's a good time to check your big-word vocabulary at the door. Unless you know the precise meaning and nuance of a big word, don't use it in your SAT essay. You're unlikely to increase your score much by using it, but *misusing* it will stand out. Always aim primarily for clarity and precision. For example, don't use *effect*, a noun, when you mean *affect*, a verb.

Ultimate Style

2. Clarity of Expression   Clarity is the key to good writing. Your thoughts may be insightful, but no one will understand them if they're not written clearly. *Clear expression* means expressing yourself in a way that makes all of your ideas easily comprehensible. Naturally, proper grammar, punctuation, and spelling will help you. But more important is the process of organizing and detailing your *thought process*. If you make vast logical leaps, jump from one subject to another, or stray from the topic, you'll sacrifice the clarity of your essay. Before you start writing, you should outline your thoughts and take the time to develop a thesis.

3. Sustained Focus   You have only twenty-five minutes to formulate, plan, write, and edit a decent first draft of an essay. You have no time or space to wander off on tangents; you must devote all your precious time and space to the task at hand. Don't get "cute" in your writing; "cute" entails taking unnecessary risks. When you're facing an SAT essay, think of a well-organized nightly news segment, not a convoluted soap opera plot.

4. Logical and Coherent Presentation of Ideas   Your essay needs to flow. You need to take a position that is supported by reasons and reinforced by examples. Each sentence should follow naturally from the last, and each paragraph should build on or add to the previous one. Structure and organization are key to creating a successful essay. Even though you have a limited amount of time, you should outline thoroughly so that your thoughts have a smooth flow, each of your arguments supports your thesis statement, and transitions carefully set up each new idea.

5. Ample Development of a Point of View   Through your point of view, you demonstrate that you understand the topic and that you have a firm opinion on it. A *developed* point of view means that your opinion isn't arbitrary—it's educated and supported by examples and reasoning. *You should have at least three solid supporting arguments in your SAT essay.* If you just restate your thesis again and again, you haven't proven it. But if you back up your claims with evidence, which can include personal or anecdotal experiences, your essay will have the power of persuasion.

6. Use of Clear Reasoning and Appropriate

Evidence   *Evidence* is another word for *examples*. If you use only abstract concepts in your essay, then your thesis hasn't been tested. But if you can use some examples to back up your arguments, then you've got something. *Appropriate* evidence is evidence that actually supports your arguments. Keep in mind that *appropriate* doesn't mean *sophisticated*. The College Board doesn't distinguish between students who have and haven't read Noam Chomsky. An example can come from a class, your personal life, a newspaper, or anything else you've read or experienced as long as it supports your argument.

Ultimate Style

Know How It's Scored

Your essay will receive a score between 1 and 6, where 6 is the highest score. You can get a 0 only if you don't write the essay or if you write about something completely unrelated to the given topic.

The SAT essays are read by a group of writing and education professionals, all of whom have gone through a rigorous training process. To prove that they know the College Board's complex scoring rubric inside and out, the readers have to read and grade approximately forty prescored essays. If they fail to give at least 70 percent of those essays the same score as the College Board's score, they're not selected as readers for the exam.

Your essay will be read and graded by two readers, which helps to ensure you won't get an unfair score by a particularly harsh reader having a bad day. Each reader will give you a score from 1 to 6, and these results will be added together for an essay subscore of between 2 and 12.

The Essay and Your Final Score   Here's how the essay fits into your overall SAT score:

- The essay counts for one-third of your final scaled Writing Score.
- The Writing Score is one-third of your final score (which is composed equally of Math, Critical Reading, and Writing).
- Therefore, the essay is one-ninth of your total SAT score.

Mathematically speaking, one-ninth isn't very much. However, since these scores are read and evaluated by college admissions committees, many of whom are the very people who pressured the College Board to create an essay section in the first place, it would behoove you to do your best to impress them.

What This Means for You   You don't have control over the scoring of your essay, since it takes place after your essay is written. But there are some scoring details that can actually help you in your quest to write a great essay:

- SAT readers know you have only twenty-five minutes, and they don't expect you to churn out a perfectly polished, carefully researched, thoroughly outlined essay. Don't spend time trying to devise an earth-shattering thesis or argument. Focus instead on nailing the fundamentals: a strong, opinionated thesis; two or three strong supporting arguments; a short but insightful conclusion; and clear writing.

- It's almost impossible to write an essay in twenty-five minutes without a grammatical or spelling error. Your essay can have a few small mistakes and still get a score of 6.

Ultimate Style

- Lofty references to obscure or sophisticated authors and books won't get you a higher score. The readers are instructed to evaluate an example only on how well it explains and supports your argument. Assuming that both examples fully support the argument, a student who quotes Aristotle will get no more points than one who recounts something unusual a friend's dog did. The College Board also likes to see diversity in your examples, so try to include examples from a variety of sources: your personal life, an article you read, a documentary you saw, a class you took, and so on.

- A long essay isn't better than a short one. It's the content of your essay that counts, not how fast you write. If your essay is short but powerful, you won't be penalized for brevity.

- There's no such thing as a "wrong answer" on the SAT essay. In fact, the readers don't really care what your opinion is, as long as you back it up with strong arguments and appropriate examples and reasoning. Don't spend any time worrying what idea is "right"—instead, determine what idea you can argue most effectively.

- The readers are instructed to reward you for what you do right rather than penalize you for what you do wrong. They're looking out for your accomplishments, not your mistakes. Do enough things right, and they'll overlook the smaller errors.

- The SAT essay is much less sophisticated and structural than an essay you'd write for class. We provide a structure as a formula so the SAT essay will be easier for you to understand; also, this formula is what graders (generally high school English teachers) are used to.

Learn the Steps

As you've seen in previous chapters, writing is but a small part of the process of creating an essay. This is no less true for the SAT essay, regardless of the time limitations. It's just as important to carefully brainstorm and outline—you'll just have to do it faster.

The time limitation probably seems both intimidating and outrageous. But keep in mind that this is not supposed to be a brilliant, polished essay: it's supposed to be a strong first draft. With that in mind, let's get down to the nitty-gritty and take a closer look at the individual steps and the time they should take:

1. Read the essay prompt   1 minute
2. Brainstorm arguments and a thesis   4 minutes
3. Outline   4 minutes
4. Write the essay   15 minutes
5. Proofread for mistakes   1 minute

1. Read the Essay Prompt   You should memorize the SAT essay instructions and requirements now so you won't have to read them again during the actual SAT. You'll save only thirty seconds or so, but you'll want that time. This way, you can skip right to the prompt, which is SAT lingo for the topic and assignment on which you're to write. This will be an excerpt from some form of written work, and it will pose a theory on a given subject. Here's our example:

Ultimate Style

> Think carefully about the quote below and the assignment that follows it:

> Time does not change us. It just unfolds us.
>
> –Max Frisch

> Do you agree with this statement? Plan and write an essay in which you develop your point of view on this issue. Support your position with reasoning and examples taken from your reading, studies, experience, or observations.

After you've read the prompt, your first task is to make sure you understand it. What specific issue is being addressed? The formal name of the issue will likely not be stated, because the

College Board wants to test your power of interpretation. In this instance, the debate seems to be about *the personal effect of time.*

Once you've identified the issue the prompt addresses, write it down in the space below the prompt. Jot down your first impressions so you can refer to them later on. You should also jot down any other immediate thoughts that come to mind. We'll return to these in the next step.

2. Brainstorm Arguments and a Thesis   Because

of the time limitation, there's no way you can brainstorm as thoroughly as we suggested in Chapter 2—but you won't have to. The topic has already been chosen, so you don't need to find an appropriate one or narrow your scope. You can also avoid the process of choosing the right side of an issue to argue. The College Board has worked hard to select a topic with two good sides for debate, and they don't care which one you choose. The important thing is that you're able to support your side with good arguments.

If you instinctively know which side of the debate you're drawn to, choose that side. This way, even if the topic doesn't interest you, your thesis can. Also, you simply won't have time to play devil's advocate and weigh the benefits of arguing each side. If, on the other hand, you're not sure which side to choose, quickly draw a brainstorming chart in the sacred space beneath the prompt and start listing arguments. For example:

Agree **Time Doesn't Change Us**	**Disagree** **Time Does Change Us**
1. Biology: doesn't change over time.	1. We're different at eighteen than we were at five—different likes, dislikes.
2. Genetic makeup guarantees who we become physically, even medically.	2. "Ugly ducklings"—takes time to become a fully formed adult, and we change into who we're meant to be.
3. Nature doesn't change radically, just slowly adapts to environmental factors.	3. Heartbreak, friendships, experiences make us who we are.
4. Evolution—the way we are has unfolded over time. We haven't "changed" without warning.	
5. Personal characteristics might strengthen or weaken, but we are always fundamentally the same people—different traits unfold but we don't change.	

Ultimate Style

We could probably come up with many more ideas, but we need only enough for our essay. Clearly, we should argue the Agree side: while we only have three arguments on the Disagree side, we have five on the Agree side.

Now that we have our arguments, we need a thesis. Because you're strapped for time, you shouldn't try to put together a carefully worded thesis statement now. We'll leave that to the writing process. Instead, just come up with a rough sentence that captures the essence of your thesis. For example:

> *Biology and genetics are a scientific way of showing that people don't actually change over time—instead, time simply unfolds them.*

3. Outline Hopefully, you still have a little space left below the essay prompt, because now you'll need it to create a quick outline. Essay outlines are universal—the structure you use for your class essays is the basically same one you'll use for the SAT essay, only the SAT version is simpler:

I. INTRODUCTION

A. Your Thesis Statement

II. BODY

A. First Major Supporting Argument
    1. Reasoning and Examples

B. Second Major Supporting Argument
    1. Reasoning and Examples

C. Third Major Supporting Argument
    1. Reasoning and Examples

III. CONCLUSION

    A. Transition to Thesis Restatement

    B. A New Perspective or Future Idea

You'll notice that there's no room in the introduction for stating your topic. Because you've already been presented with a topic, you won't need to introduce it, and writing the extra one or two sentences will take time away from more important resources. Likewise, transitions should be kept to a minimum. A single word such as *additionally, furthermore,* or *finally* will serve as an indicator that you're moving on to a new thought without taking too much time to write.

Looking at our brainstorming chart, we need to figure out which ideas are supporting arguments, and which are reasons and examples. Once we've done that, we can insert them into our outline in the correct order, always keeping in mind the golden rule: start with the most compelling argument and end with the least. Also, keep in mind that you may come up with additional arguments as you write your outline—don't feel limited by your brainstorming chart.

Ultimate Style

Our outline now looks like this:

I. INTRODUCTION

A. Thesis Statement: Biology and genetics are a scientific way of showing that people don't actually change over time—instead, time simply unfolds them.

II. BODY

A. Biology and Genes
  1. Physical traits: we inherit from our parents
  2 Personality traits: inherit from parents
  3. Medicines can help with medical problems, but there's no way to change biology
  4. Traits can be dormant or apparent, but they don't just appear out of thin air

B. The Natural World

    1. Nothing really changes—rivers smooth out rocks, but the rocks are still rocks

    2. Water turns to ice, but is still water

    3. The seasons are on a cycle that doesn't change

C. Personal Experience

    1. Smoking—Dad wanted to quit, tried for years, finally successful but still craved cigarettes

    2. He didn't "change"—but his determination to quit unfolded

    3. His habits changed, but he didn't

    4. Effect of love?

III. CONCLUSION

A. Thesis Restatement: connect to Dad's smoking—time unfolded him, didn't change him

B. Expand thesis to larger point or relate to another area (optional)—effect of love?

You can see that we thought of more evidence as we outlined, and we didn't use everything from our brainstorming chart. That's fine. You can change and add ideas as you go. Also, the idea of the "effect of love" appears in two places—we can decide where to put it later on, or just throw it out altogether. Again, we can change our mind as we go.

    Obviously, the outline we've provided above won't fit in the tiny space you're provided to plan. Ours has been written out thoroughly enough so that you can understand it. When you create your own outline, you should write only as much as you need to understand it. No one else will read it.

4. Write the Essay   Once your organize your thoughts, you'll have to write—fast. You have fifteen minutes.

5. Proofread for Mistakes   If leaving only one minute for proofreading seems like a very short time, that's because it's the least important step. As we mentioned, a few small mistakes aren't going to rob you of that coveted 6. In fact, you might think of proofreading as an optional step. If you find you're finished with your essay before time is up, go back and proofread. But don't allow yourself to write a sloppy and incomplete conclusion just to have one extra minute for a review.

If you do make time to proofread, look for the usual suspects:

- Grammar
- Spelling
- Punctuation

No matter what you correct, be sure to do it quickly and neatly. A misspelled word is better than one that's been scribbled out and rewritten illegibly above it. Likewise, you won't be able to reorganize your thoughts or restructure sentences. It would simply make your paper messy and indecipherable to the readers. Stay focused on the small stuff that you really can improve upon in a very short amount of time.

SAT Essay in Action

With only fifteen minutes, we don't have much time to write a perfect essay. But we do have time to write one with a strong argument and solid ideas. Here's what we came up with:

> While it's often said that someone has become "a changed man" and that people in general "change over time," these statements are actually somewhat misleading. If we look at the effect of time on people and carefully consider factors such as biology, the rules of nature, and individual experience, it quickly becomes apparent that time does not change people; rather, it unfolds them.
>
> Thanks to major advancements in the field of genetic biology, it is now common knowledge that the genes inherited from one's parents play an enormous role in a person's fundamental attributes. Not only do genes determine a person's race, eye color, and other physical features, they can also determine personality traits, such as intelligence, propensity toward substance abuse, artistic aptitude, temperament, and even sexual preference. While these tendencies and attributes may lie dormant in a person for years, they still exist in his or her biological makeup; the question is not if they exist, but when they manifest themselves. To say that time actually changes a person, then, dismisses the role of genetic biology. It suggests that a person sheds certain traits and acquires others over a period of weeks, months, or years as if out of thin air. A more scientifically sound notion is that traits often remain folded up inside a person, only to reveal themselves (become unfolded) over a period of time.

While biology provides many answers to the nature of human life, it's equally as important to consider our context in the natural world around us. Nature, it turns out, provides us very few examples of actual change. Rivers, for instance, may flow over rocks and pebbles for countless years, but this process does not change rocks into other objects; it slowly smoothes and molds rocks into slightly different shapes. Likewise, the river may turn to ice in the winter, but this, too, is not change. The ice is still composed of water, simply in a different form. This is all part of a natural cycle that affects most of the earth and its creatures, as witnessed on a small scale in seasonal variations, or on a larger scale in evolution. Since we, too, are part of nature, it seems unlikely that vastly different principles would govern our development and evolution than would govern the rest of the world we inhabit.

As if scientific evidence were not enough to cast doubt upon the notion of people changing over time, there is the further consideration of personal experience. My father was a smoker for sixteen years, and spent the last three of those years eager to quit. He tried to quit numerous times over those three years, and finally was successful with the use of nicotine patches. While he has now gone without tobacco for two years and is happy that he has quit, he has not "changed." He still craves cigarettes every day, and says he probably will until he dies. He still struggles with self-restraint, as he did before he quit. While he now has the determination to refrain from smoking, his determination in other aspects of his life has remained more or less the same. In other words, while his daily habits have changed over time, he has not. The traits he now *exhibits are ones he had all along, he's just working harder to put them into action. Time did not change him; it unfolded his existing determination far enough that he was able to cease a single behavior.*

Commentary   Our essay isn't perfect—with only fifteen minutes to write, it can't be. However, the essay succeeds in developing a point of view, presenting ideas logically, and using sound reasoning to back up our claims—all with clarity and precision of language. We didn't have time to write an actual "conclusion," but in this essay, we didn't really need to—the evidence we'd presented successfully argued our thesis, and restating our point of view would have been repetitive. The main goals have been achieved, and this essay would receive a good score.

The College Admissions Essay

College admissions essays and academic essays possess fundamentally distinct characteristics. In academic essays, you try to avoid the word "I." In admissions essays, "I" is the topic. Academic essays require you to be opinionated and argumentative. Admissions essays require you to demonstrate you're neither. And while instructors use academic essays to see what you've learned *in* class, admissions officers are most interested to see what you've learned *outside* of class.

Many of the tools you've learned here will help you to write a strong college admissions essay. Good writing, solid structure, analytical thought—you'll need to have them all. Along with those essentials, however, you have to include a great deal of *yourself.* Perfect grammar, strong structure, and deep thinking will only get you so far—what admissions committees want to see more than anything else is *you.*

Meet the Admissions Committee

While colleges have their fair share of gravel-voiced old men and women wearing wool suits and thick glasses, these people tend to be professors, not members of admissions committees.

Professors can be as cantankerous as they please—but admissions committees must be in touch with eighteen-year-old students. Your readers will be generally composed of fair, even-tempered, relatively young people. Many colleges even hire recent graduates as the first wave of admissions readers. These twentysomethings read numerous applications and pass the best ones on to the next level, associate directors. The associate directors read these applications and then pass their top picks on to an admissions director, who makes the final decision.

Ultimate Style

Be Yourself

Colleges don't expect every student to be a multitalented, all-American football captain or class president. Just look at the pictures in a college brochure: a diverse student body composed of young people from all walks of life, with many different interests and life experiences. Admissions directors are well aware of this need for diversity, and their jobs depend on recruiting a varied array of artists, athletes, computer whizzes, intellectuals, and tree-huggers. So don't make yourself sound like something you're not. Embrace who you are—there's always a place for you.

Understand the Admissions Essay's Role

You've heard the saying, "You can't judge a book by its cover." This adage applies to people as well as books: the important part is what's underneath the surface. The admissions essay allows you to show what's *inside* you, beyond what the committee can determine from the classes you've taken, your GPA, your SAT and AP scores, and your name/race/age/social security number. Grades and scores are important, but they say nothing about what kind of person you are. Intellectual curiosity, unique perspectives, creativity, interests, and life experiences mean a great deal to colleges. They are the indicators of maturity and potential collegiate success. None of this can be found in standardized test scores or grades, but it can be found in the pages of your essay—as long as you know what to write and, just as important, what *not* to write.

Know What *Not* to Write

Before we get to what you should write in your admissions essays, let's examine what you *shouldn't* write. We've put together a list of the four most common flawed essay types:

1. The resumay
2. The world traveler's account
3. The tale of the super-rounded student
4. The "How I Saved the World" essay

1. The Resumay   A *resumay* is a "résumé-essay," and admissions committees see them all the time. Resumays are just like résumés, but they're written in prose form. They detail every single academic accomplishment the student has ever achieved, usually in chronological order. Resumays have two big problems:

- Every accomplishment they name can be found elsewhere in the application. The admissions committee already knows you got a 3.7 GPA, took AP English, and were president of the chess club, so telling them again is a waste of time.

- Resumays are focused entirely upon the accomplishment instead of the insight gained from it. Every chess club president from every high school across America is applying to college too. What makes you more interesting than them?

Ultimate Style

2. The World Traveler's Account   The world traveler is the student who—you guessed it—has traveled the world. Not just once, but many times, often on a unicycle. There's nothing wrong with traveling, of course. It's a wonderful opportunity and can provide fresh perspectives on the world. However, the world traveler is usually so busy naming every place he or she has been that he or she forgets to describe what lessons or knowledge the experience delivered. You're unlikely to impress an admissions committee with the number of places you've been. They've probably traveled a bit themselves. You're better off focusing on one specific destination and the effect it has had on your outlook on life.

As a side note—if you haven't traveled the world, don't worry. Few young people have. The important thing is what you've done with the experiences you *have* had. Consider these two opening sentences:

In the summer of my junior year, I climbed Mt. Kilimanjaro, the highest peak in Africa.

In the summer of my junior year, I climbed a small hill in Iowa, looked out over the vast expanse of land, and realized that I must become a geologist so I can understand the wonder of the world around me.

Which statement interested you the most? The second, of course, because the writer expressed a perspective, not just an experience.

3. The Tale of the Super-Rounded Student   There's football after school, volunteering at the soup kitchen on Mondays, guitar practice on Wednesdays, membership in Amnesty International, and a part in the school musical. And that's just the fall semester. Having numerous interests is fine, and being well-rounded is certainly a virtue. But nothing tops having *a sustained passion in one area*. Rather than listing every activity you're involved in, focus on one and describe what it means to you. You might ask yourself the following questions:

1. How has it changed your life?
2. What have you learned?
3. What kind of experiences have you had in one club, sport, or hobby?
4. What was the most significant moment, and why?
5. What challenges have you faced and overcome?

Don't worry if you're not the most well-rounded student. You're not expected to be involved in sports, music, theater, three or four clubs, and numerous volunteer activities, regardless of what you've heard. Do you think Einstein's success was hindered by the fact that he didn't play rugby after changing the world of physics every day?

4. The "How I Saved the World" Essay You've organized clothing drives, worked in soup kitchens, protested outside your local mayor's office, raised money for AIDS awareness, and now—*obviously*—you're going to turn these accomplishments into your college application essay. Not so fast. High school students today are getting involved in community service in record numbers, and "how I saved the world" essays are a dime a dozen. College admissions committees often raise their eyebrows when they see this type of essay, since some students do service solely for the purpose of having material to write about for their application. This is especially likely if they didn't begin doing service until their junior year of high school. Another problem is that, all too often, these essays detail elaborate service projects or volunteer experiences without delving deeper into what those experiences *meant* to the applicant.

If you plan to write an essay that describes an experience you had with community service, you need to take certain precautions to ensure that your essay doesn't fall into this danger zone of insincerity. Instead of simply bragging about what great things you did, go deeper into the experience by asking yourself these questions:

Ultimate Style

- How has it changed your life?
- What have you learned about others?
- What have you learned about your own self or life?
- What was the most significant moment, and why?
- How do you think this experience may influence your life path, if it will?

As with any essay, you need to make it *personal*. The admissions committee wants to see self-reflection that goes beyond "I'm a good person, see?"

Flaunt What Matters

As we said, the purpose of the college admissions essay is to reveal the qualities and experiences that don't come through in a résumé or application form. While there's no limit to the potential qualities you can boast, the ones that will most impress an admissions committee are the following:

1. Self-awareness
2. Curiosity
3. Possessing life experience
4. A history of sustained passions
5. Strong writing skills

Let's take a look at these qualities in a little more detail to better understand just what admissions committees want.

1. Self-Awareness   The four types of flawed essays we listed earlier all lacked self-awareness. The writers were certainly aware of what they had done, but they showed no awareness of what they had learned, how they had grown, or what perspective they had gained. Proving that you've thought about your life and experiences will score more points than the experiences themselves.

A critical aspect of self-awareness is the ability to recognize changes in yourself. Perhaps you used to be shy and withdrawn, but performing in the school play brought out your true colors. Or maybe you took material things for granted until you got an after-school job. Remember that not every life experience you write about has to be an accomplishment. Describing a failure that led you to turn over a new leaf or improve your performance will demonstrate humility while still showing you're now a strong candidate.

Ultimate Style

2. Curiosity   In many ways, curiosity is the opposite of contentment. People who are content continue to do the same thing over and over again, demonstrating little drive or initiative. Curious people, on the other hand, seek out new things, always eager to learn, discover, and create. Curiosity is the quality that leads people to read a book on something they know nothing about, learn a foreign language, try a new sport, and seek out solutions to various problems. This quality is important to colleges. While you're required to take classes, do your homework, and participate in class discussions in high school, you're free to do whatever you please in college.

Possessing curiosity will ensure that you make the most of your time and continue to strive for success after you graduate.

If you haven't read every book, played every sport, or designed bizarre inventions for the science fair, it doesn't mean colleges will think you're overly content. Essays give you a great opportunity to demonstrate curiosity by discussing your passion for something specific. Even a hobby as simple as collecting CDs can prove your curiosity if you demonstrate how important the passion is to you and how it has changed your life.

3. Possessing Life Experience   *Life experience* doesn't have to mean only significant accomplishments. Not everyone has the opportunity to backpack across the Rockies or live in a foreign country. A life experience can be something very mundane, something tragic, or simply something that had a huge effect on *you*. Many excellent essays have focused on a grueling summer job, parents' divorce, the death of a loved one, or a part-time volunteer activity. As always, the scope and prominence of the experience is much less important than what you've learned from it. What admissions committees really want to see is that you've struggled and learned, failed and fought back, taken on challenges, and developed a view on life.

4. A History of Sustained Passions   We all know someone who has a new favorite thing every two weeks. Last month it was tennis, which then became horseback riding. That was fun until ballet was discovered, which was absolutely *the best* until it got really boring and a new karate studio opened up down the street. Sound familiar? Having many interests is a positive quality. But jumping from one activity to another suggests that you're never satisfied and perhaps lack the ability to stick it out when the going gets tough.

A sustained passion is one you have stuck to for a year or longer, and whether you're highly successful or just mediocre, your enthusiasm keeps you going. If you're someone who tends to jump from one passion to the next, you shouldn't lie about the length of your involvement. Instead, focus on the one activity that means the most to you, and describe how it has changed your outlook or perspective.

Ultimate Style

5. Strong Writing Skills   Every essay, regardless of type, requires good writing skills. The admissions essay is no different, but it does allow for more flexibility. While your academic essays are expected to be somewhat formal, you're permitted to use a slightly more free-spirited, colloquial tone in admissions essays. Demonstrating life experience, maturity, and insight is ultimately more important than a fancy vocabulary and stunning sentence structure, and if your uniqueness really shines, it can easily eclipse otherwise pedestrian writing skills.

Know the Most Common Questions

With literally hundreds of colleges and universities scattered across North America, it's impossible for us to cover every possible essay you could be required to write. While some schools ask you to answer one specific question, others require you to choose three topics from a longer list. Some schools leave it all up to you, requesting that you write about whatever you please. Over the years, however, a few topics for admissions essays have emerged as the most frequently and widely used. We've compiled the six most common ones. They are:

1. Evaluate a significant experience, achievement, risk you have taken, or ethical dilemma you have faced, and discuss its impact on you.

2. Discuss some issue of personal, local, national, or international concern and its importance to you.

3. Indicate a person who has had a significant influence on you, and describe that influence.

4. Describe a character in fiction, an historical figure, or a creative work (art, music, film, etc.) that has had an influence upon you, and explain that influence.

5. A range of academic interests, personal perspectives, and life experiences adds much to the educational mix. Given your personal background, describe an experience that illustrates what you would bring to the diversity in a college community, or an encounter that demonstrated the importance of diversity to you.

6. Write on any topic of your choice.

If you're drawing a blank on how you'd answer any of these questions, don't worry. After all, your essay serves as your "face" to the admissions committee, and you want to put your best face forward. Having to choose only one aspect of your entire life to represent you as a person is a difficult challenge. Just remember that everyone has many fascinating experiences and unusual qualities. The trick is identifying them, and the best way to do this is to brainstorm.

Brainstorming a Topic   When we brainstormed for academic essays, we wanted to come up with a suitable and appropriate topic for discussion. In the admissions essay, *you* are ultimately the topic, and you can use the brainstorming process to look over your life, discover who you are, and decide what aspect best sells you to the admissions committee. We've included a brainstorming worksheet at the end of this chapter that you can use to jog your memory and find the best subject for your essay.

Ultimate Style

Understand the Structure

Every essay has the basic structure of Introduction-Body-Conclusion. This never changes, just as every movie you see has a Beginning-Middle-End. However, in a college admissions essay, the division of the body into three (or more) distinct arguments that all support the thesis is occasionally modified. This most frequently occurs when the purpose of an essay is to tell a narrative, portray a cause and effect relationship, or demonstrate a before-and-after scenario. In these cases, the overall structure of the essay may change somewhat to best render the significance of the experience you're discussing.

What follows is a quick and dirty sampling of some alternate structures. We cover three types:

1. The chronological structure
2. The half & half
3. The three elements

We'll explain each of these and provide examples of when and where they might be used. We've chosen examples that aren't necessarily intuitive in order to demonstrate how adaptable each structure can potentially be. For example, the chronological structure would be just as well suited to describe an experience as it would to describe a person. The best structure is the one that suits your particular take on the topic. We wish simply to present you with possibilities that may help you figure out your strategy. You may want to try to outline your essay in a few different ways, and then choose which one works best for you.

The Chronological Structure   In the standard essay structure, you use the introduction to lay out your topic and present a thesis. In the body, you present arguments that support your thesis. In the conclusion, you summarize and suggest where your ideas might go next. However, some admissions essay questions aren't really looking for a thesis that you would attempt to prove. Most of them, in fact, are asking you to choose a specific topic (a fictional character, experience, or role model), and then discuss the impact or influence it's had on you. You might choose a chronological structure to address this kind of question. Here, the topic is the person/experience, the thesis is the effect on you, and the three (or so) paragraphs of the body are used to describe the narrative of your experience, using a before-during-after chronology.

Chronological Structure In Action   To illustrate the concept of a chronological essay structure, let's look at a potential structure for an essay describing the effect of a role model (let's say it's a basketball coach named Coach Robbins):

I. INTRODUCTION

A   Introducing the topic—Coach Robbins

B. Thesis—Coach Robbins taught me the importance of teamwork.

II. BODY

A. First stage (Before I met Coach Robbins)

   1. Three examples of team status before meeting

      a. Our basketball team played badly.

      b. Our team didn't get along; we fought and bickered.

      c. I didn't enjoy playing basketball.

B. Second stage (Coach Robbins became our new coach)

   1. Three examples of my early experience with him

      a. He forced us to practice very late.

  b. He made us do cheesy bonding exercises with teammates.

  c. I didn't like him; he was too tough and demanding.

 C. Third stage (Coach Robbins's lesson has its effect)

  1. Three examples of the lesson learned

   a. We began winning games.

   b. I began to trust and respect my teammates, as well as enjoy their company outside basketball.

   c. Our understanding of teamwork led us to win the championship.

III. CONCLUSION

A. Restating thesis—Now I understand teamwork.

B. New thought—It has helped me to understand the value of cooperation in school, in the workplace, and within my family.

Granted, the details of this outline are ridiculously hackneyed (no fewer than ten movies tell the same story). However, the outline succeeds in capturing the essence of the essay topic. There is narrative and drama, the focus is on both the role model and the student, and we fully understand the life lesson learned.

The Half & Half The half & half has a structure that is, as the name suggests, split in half. It's usually used to describe a cause-and-effect or before-and-after relationship. In the cause-and-effect example, the first half of the essay focuses on the cause, and the second half focuses on the effect it had on you. In the instance of a before-and-after relationship, half of the essay focuses on what you were like before an experience, event, or encounter, and the other half focuses on what you were like afterward. The key to the half & half structure is not giving too much importance to the catalyst. Remember that *you* are ultimately the topic, and *your viewpoint* is what counts. Don't get so caught up in describing the experience that you forget your own role in it.

Half & Half Structure in Action   For an example of the half & half, let's use the cause-and-effect approach and answer the common question about a significant life experience, achievement, or risk. We'll discuss the experience of being an exchange student in Japan (a country that some Americans find to have outdated gender roles, and that—due to its ethnic homogeneity—sometimes views foreigners as minorities).

I. INTRODUCTION

A. Introducing the topic—Exchange student program in Japan.

B. Thesis—I learned a great deal about the life of women and minorities outside my own country.

II. BODY

A. Discussion of the cause

    1. History of my trip to Japan

2. I had never traveled; took my lifestyle for granted; filled with fear

3. A few significant experiences (being treated as a minority, unfair expectations of me as a woman in Japan)

4. My impressions of and reactions to the culture, country, people

B. Discussion of the effect and history of my life since

   1. History of my life since returning to America; the changes in my life

     a. I am now more worldly; no longer apprehensive, don't take things for granted.

     b. I have a different view of minorities and foreigners; volunteer at ESL school for recent immigrants.

     c. I have started a blog for women to discuss their treatment in various countries across the world.

III. CONCLUSION

A. Restating thesis—I have come to better understand myself and the role/treatment of women throughout the world, thus . . .

B. New thought—I want to be an International Studies major and improve the lives of women worldwide by bringing attention to treatment/status across the globe.

This structure succeeds as a half & half since we don't spend too much time on the experience itself. The focus of the essay is on *our own role* in that experience. We are the topic, not the experience of living in Japan.

The Three Elements   The three elements structure is very similar to the standard essay structure. Each of the body's three supporting paragraphs is used to focus on individual thoughts, all of which pertain to the thesis. Instead of arguments, however, the body contains "elements"—distinct aspects of the topic that have led to your thesis. Think of it this way: instead of arguing each point, you're describing each point in detail, in a way that gives a vivid picture of who you are.

Ultimate Style

Three Elements Structure in Action   To clarify the three elements essay, let's make an outline for an essay on a historical figure who has influenced us. We chose John Lennon and have used each supporting paragraph to identify a different aspect we admire: musical ability, political activism, and an outspoken, unwavering self-assurance.

I. INTRODUCTION

A. Introducing the topic—John Lennon

B. Thesis—Lennon has influenced me in my work, art, and perspective on life.

II. BODY

 A. First element (Lennon's music and lyrics)

    1. Three aspects of his music and their effect on me

        a. As a musician, I have been influenced by Lennon's innovative lyrics and songwriting; have strived to write thoughtful work.

        b. Lennon's music had social conscience and influenced popular thought.

        c. I have come to believe in the positive influence art can make on culture.

B. Second element (Lennon's political activism)

    1. Three aspects of his activism and effect on me

        a. Lennon's antiwar message during Vietnam

        b. I was inspired to become more involved in community and volunteer groups for social justice.

        c. I headed local chapter to raise money for aid to Afghan refugees during war on terror in 2002.

C. Third element (Lennon's self-assurance)

    1. Three aspects of this and how it's influenced me

        a. Lennon was known as stubborn and unrelenting, and his statements often got him in trouble/created controversy.

        b. I've been inspired to speak out about what I feel is right and not "tow the party line" for popularity, profit.

        c. Egotism and stubbornness are not virtues, but I want to strive for balance and fairness while still pursuing what's right .

III. CONCLUSION

A. Restating thesis—How Lennon has led me to become a better person.

B. New thought—I want to be a person who can also provide art, music, and a positive message for society.

There are two potential pitfalls of this planned essay that relate to content. First, focusing on a pop-culture figure is risky, as it can seem like nothing more than "hero worship." Make sure the person you choose has enough worthwhile qualities and isn't just "cool." Second, remember that the admissions committee wants to get to know you, not someone else. Notice how in each of the elements above, we've emphasized what *we've* learned and *our* actions. This isn't a biography!

Ultimate Style

Write the Essay

The rules of writing an academic essay apply to college admissions essays as well. In a nutshell, you must punctuate well, use proper grammar, and follow every other rule you've heard a thousand times. In the eyes of the admissions committee, you've had your entire life to master writing skills, and they won't tolerate mistakes. Proofread thoroughly, but more important, refine your essay through numerous drafts. Show it to friends, family members, and teachers. Spending an entire semester developing an essay is not uncommon for college-bound students.

You should remember six things as you begin writing your essay:

1. You are the topic.
2. Make your essay stand out.
3. Emphasize strengths the application overlooks.
4. Use humor wisely.
5. Be descriptive.
6. Stick to the topic.

1. You Are the Topic   Even when an admissions essay asks you to discuss another person, it's you the committee really wants to get to know. A role model, character, life event, or issue is just a tactic admissions committees use to focus your scope on one aspect of your life, thus minimizing the chance that you'll start your life story at age two. Therefore, always connect every experience, person, or issue back to you by discussing the effect upon you, similarities to you, or path you have chosen since the encounter. If you've written more than three sentences in a row without self-reference, you've probably lost your focus.

2. Make Your Essay Stand Out   Admissions committees read literally thousands of essays over the period of a few weeks, so it's vital that yours stands out. You don't have to be the smartest or most-accomplished student, but *every detail you can include will make you specific as a person.* Use your essay to paint a picture of yourself. Make yourself familiar and intimate. The more people feel they know you, the more difficult it will

be to say no to admitting you. Fill your writing with the kind
of subtleties and nuances that make you original, and never be
afraid to wear your uniqueness on your sleeve.

3. Emphasize Strengths Your Application
Overlooks
If you have a great GPA and strong SAT scores,
don't worry about proving you're smart. Instead, use your
essay to show that you're an interesting individual. If you don't
have many passions, describe why the one you do have is so
important to you. If your academic accomplishments aren't as
great as you think they could be, you should feel free to explain
why (but don't make excuses). Weaknesses are acceptable;
whining is not.

Ultimate Style

4. Use Humor Wisely
Humor can be a great gift. But
if you use it inappropriately, it will backfire. Never sacrifice
honesty and sincerity for a joke. The best humor in admissions
essays is either observational or self-mocking. Antiestablish-
ment, jaded, or cynical humor can paint a portrait that you are
holier than thou or too cool for words. Likewise, adopting an
irreverent tone for your entire essay will seem disrespectful to
the admissions committee. Remember that the best humor is
always in the details.

5. Be Descriptive
We guarantee that 50 percent of the
admissions essays written every year begin with some form of
the following: "For my essay, I'm going to discuss my relationship with John Sanders, an English teacher and role model
who has taught me the value of literature." *Boring.* Spice things

up by pulling your audience in with descriptive passages. They create drama, accentuate narrative, and get the reader's attention immediately. The more vivid an image you can put into the minds of the admissions committee, the more they will feel they know you.

6. Stick to the Topic   If an application requires you to write on a specific topic, don't surprise them with something else. They won't be amused. However, if you're invited to write on "a topic of your choice," you should feel free to, as long as it's special and something that couldn't be woven into another essay question.

Application Essay in Action

This is an actual admissions essay written by a student named Soraya Palmer, Connecticut College Class of 2001. After the essay are a few comments and notes about what the writer did right.

PROMPT: Evaluate a significant experience, achievement, risk you have taken, or ethical dilemma you have faced and its impact on you.

Finding Truths

In my life, I have taken many journeys without which I would not have experienced important truths. My father started us off early, taking us on many journeys to help us understand that true knowledge comes only from experience. We took trips every winter break to Madrid, Mexico, Costa Rica, and to Jamaica and Trinidad, my parents' homeland, for Christmas. Silly things I remember from those trips include the mango chili sauce on the pork in Maui, the names of the women who gave out the towels by the pools in Selva Verde, Costa Rica, eating dinner at 10 p.m. in Spain. These were all tourist experiences that I, at first, found spellbinding. My truths were the truths of the tourist brochures: beautiful hotels, beaches, and cities. I did not see the blindfolds. I did not appreciate how being held hostage by the beauty of the surface—the beaches and cities—blinded me to the absence of Puerto Rican natives on the streets of San Juan; I did not understand how the prevalence and familiarity of English conspired to veil the beauty of the Spanish language beneath volumes of English translations.

I learned more about these truths in my sophomore year of high school, when I was among a group of students selected to visit Cuba. My grandmother was born in Cuba, yet I had never thought to research my own heritage. I have remained the naïve American who saw Castro as some distant enemy of my country, accepting this as fact because this seemed to be the accepted wisdom. I soon became intrigued, however, with this supposed plague to my freedom, my culture, and everything good and decent. I began to think, just what is communism anyway? What's so bad about Castro and

Cuba—and I hear they have good coffee. I believed that what was missing was a lack of understanding between our two cultures, and that acceptance of our differences would come only with knowledge.

My first impression of Cuba was the absence of commercialism. I saw no giant golden arch enticing hungry Cubans with beef-laced fries; I did see billboards of Che Guevara and signposts exhorting unity and love. I realized, however, that much of the uniqueness that I relished here might be gone if the trade blockades in Cuba were ever lifted. The parallels and the irony were not lost on me. I was stepping out of an American political cave that shrouded the beauty of Cuba and stepping into another, one built on patriotic socialism, one where truths were just as ideological as, yet very different from, mine.

History, I recognized, is never objective. The journeys I have taken have been colored by my prior experiences and by what my feelings were in those moments. Everyone holds a piece of the truth. Maybe facts don't matter. Perhaps my experience is my truth and the more truths I hear from everyone else, the closer I will get to harmonization. Maybe there is no harmony, and I must go through life challenging and being challenged, perhaps finding perspectives from which I can extract—but never call—truth. I must simply find ways to understand others, to seek in them what is common to us all and perhaps someday find unity in our common human bond. This is what life has taught me so far, my sum of truths gleaned from experiencing many cultures. I don't know if these truths will hold, but I hope that my college experience will be like my trip to Cuba—challenging some truths, strengthening others, and helping me experience new ones.

Commentary   This essay is an excellent example of how to tackle the "significant experience" topic. It starts off strong, with a sentence that tells us exactly what we'll encounter in the essay: the writer has taken many journeys, but it's the *impact* of those journeys that she'll ultimately reveal. This keeps the essay from falling into the dangerous "world traveler" category. The writer uses specific details, such as food and other attractions, to create a vivid picture of her journeys. What makes this essay excellent, however, is the writer's obvious self-awareness. By showing how her truths changed from the "truths of the tourist brochures" to more complicated, political, and cultural truths, she demonstrates a mature perspective and reveals that she is capable of deep self-reflection.

Throughout the essay, the writer is careful to keep the focus on herself—she doesn't spend a lot of time describing her journeys, analyzing the complexities of communism, or providing background on the relationship between Cuba and the United States. Instead, she focuses on her own thoughts, perspectives, learning, and experiences—which is what an admissions committee cares about most.

The writer has used a chronological structure, describing her experiences and the thoughts they spurred roughly in the order in which they occurred. Her narrative begins with the

Ultimate Style

journeys she took as a child, goes on to detail more complex, mature journeys, then concludes with a larger idea about the impact her experiences have had. This is an effective structure to show her changing perspective.

Brainstorming Worksheet

Depending on where you are in your academic career, it may be too soon to start writing your college admissions essay. After all, if you're only a sophomore in high school, you still have many books, classes, and life experiences ahead that will shape who you are. However, it's never too soon to start brainstorming, so take some time to fill out our brainstorming worksheet. It will help you to start generating some ideas and provide you with a new context in which to view things you do between now and college application time. Furthermore, if you have a few years before college, you can return to your worksheet later and have concrete evidence of how you used to think, act, and view the world, as well as how other people viewed you. This will serve as a road map of your development, which will ultimately help you to discover how you've become the person you are.

Write your answers in the space provided or on a separate sheet of paper.

Section One: Self-Discovery

Name at least two role models who possess qualities you strive to emulate, and why.

_____

_____

_____

_____

_____

_____

_____

_____

Ultimate Style

What political or ethical issue makes you the most angry? Why?

_____

_____

_____

_____

_____

_____

_____

_____

What political or ethical issue has inspired you to change your own lifestyle or the world around you? Explain.

_____

_____

_____

_____

_____

_____

_____

_____

What creative work (fine art, music, film, writing) do you find yourself returning to most often when you need comfort, excitement, relaxation, or meditation? Why this work?

_____

_____

_____

_____

_____

_____

_____

_____

If you could have lived the life of any fictional character from a book, whose would it be? Why?

_____

_____

_____

_____

_____

_____

_____

On what philosophy, religion, academic field, or issue do you think you have a unique perspective? Explain your perspective.

_____

_____

_____

_____

_____

_____

_____

What has been the hardest period or event in your life to get through? Why?

_____

_____

_____

_____

_____

_____

_____

_____

What has always stood out in your mind as the most humiliating or embarrassing mistake you have made over the past five years?

_____

_____

_____

_____

_____

_____

_____

_____

Name three accomplishments, choices, or decisions about which you are most proud, whether you were recognized or not.

_____

_____

_____

_____

_____

_____

_____

Ultimate Style

Name one positive and one negative misconception you think people have about you before they get to know you well.

Positive

_____

_____

_____

Negative

_____

_____

_____

Looking back at who you were three years ago, in what way do you think you've changed the most?

_____

_____

_____

_____

_____

_____

_____

_____

Section Two: An Outside Perspective

For this section, you should ask close friends or family members for their thoughts, and record them in the lines provided.

Ask two close friends or family members to name three adjectives that describe you.

Person One   **Person Two**

1 _____   1 _____

_____   _____

Ultimate
Style   2 _____   2 _____

_____   _____

3 _____   3 _____

_____   _____

Ask two close friends or family members to name a time they were most proud of you.

Person One
_____

_____

_____

Person Two
_____

_____

_____

Ask two close friends or family members to list your three greatest strengths.

Person One   Person Two

1 _____   1 _____

  _____   _____

2 _____   2 _____

  _____   _____

3 _____   3 _____

  _____   _____

Ask two close friends or family members to name two times in *your* life that they will never forget.

Person One

_____

_____

_____

Person Two

_____

_____

_____

Once you have finished filling out the brainstorming worksheet, you should take a little time away from it. Don't expect the perfect topic to come to you instantly.

Crash Course in Grammar

Good writing is vital to the success of an essay. Grammar, spelling, punctuation, and errors distract readers from your argument and negatively affect your credibility as a writer, while good writing can encourage your readers to trust you. Correct grammar, spelling, and punctuation aren't of utmost importance in an SAT essay, since you have so little time to write and proofread. In all other essays, however, you should take care to scrutinize these matters in the revision process. When you have time to write and revise carefully, there's no excuse for sloppy writing.

It's not always easy to identify errors in your writing, and it takes practice to know how to correct them. But the more you know about grammar basics, the easier it will be for you to read your work closely and pinpoint areas where you writing needs help.

Make Subjects and Verbs Agree

A singular subject (such as *puppy*) requires a singular verb (*plays*); a plural subject (*puppies*) requires a plural verb (*play*). This is pretty easy, but it can get confusing when your subject is a collective noun (such as *family, group, team,* or *class*). A collective noun implies more than one person but is considered singular and takes a singular verb:

> *The family hopes to find a house by the ocean.*

Certain things that go together seem plural but are actually singular:

> *Peanut butter and jelly is my favorite sandwich.*

Also, the words *each, either, neither, everyone, nobody, somebody,* and *no one* are singular and require a singular verb:

> *Nobody likes learning the rules of grammar.*

Make Pronouns and Antecedents Agree

An *antecedent* is the thing or person a pronoun refers to. When you use a pronoun, make sure it agrees with its antecedent. If the antecedent is singular (*Whitney*), use a singular pronoun (*he*). If the antecedent is plural (*friends*), use a plural pronoun (*they*).

Problems arise when you're not sure whether or not to use a masculine or feminine pronoun. Take a look at this sentence:

> *A writer strives to entertain and inform his readers.*

Writer is the antecedent, and *his* is the pronoun—and even though the antecedent and pronoun are both singular, the *his* isn't exactly right. How do we know the writer is a man? You may have learned that you should use masculine pronouns (*he, him, his*) as "universal" pronouns that can apply to both females and males, but this is a bit outdated, and many instructors prefer that you do otherwise. You should make an effort to use pronouns that do not assume one gender or the other. Take a look at how we can rewrite our sentence:

A writer strives to entertain and inform his or her readers.

Since this sentence refers to a writer in general, we've used the phrase *his or her* as the pronoun. However, using both pronouns can sometimes be wordy and awkward. There's a better way to revise this sentence:

Writers strive to entertain and inform their readers.

If you rewrite the sentence to make the antecedent (*writers*) plural, you can use a plural pronoun (*they*), and therefore avoid the whole problem.

Use Pronouns Clearly

Don't make your reader guess the meaning of a pronoun. It should always be clear who *it, they, she, he, him,* or *her* is. Consider the following sentence:

*My dad met with the coach, and he told him that I was having
health problems.*

Who is *he*? Who is *him*? Instead, revise the sentence for clarity:

*My dad met with the coach, and he told the coach that I was
having health problems.*

Use Words Correctly

There are many tricky words that you may misuse in your essay
without even realizing it. Be sure to look carefully through your
work to make sure you haven't fallen into any sneaky language
traps.

It's* vs. *Its   *It's* is a contraction, meaning "it is." *Its* is a
possessive pronoun (*The television series is in its final season*).
Possessive pronouns (*his, hers, whose, its, ours, theirs*, or *yours*)
do not take apostrophes.

Affect* vs. *Effect   *Affect* is a verb, meaning "to influence":

The death of my grandmother affected me deeply.

The word *affect* can also be used as a noun, but you will almost
never use it this way.

Effect can be a verb or a noun. As a noun, it means "result"; as
a verb, it means "to bring about":

The presidential debates had an effect on the outcome of the election.

As president of student council, I effected significant change.

Appraise vs. Apprise   To *appraise* is to figure out the value of something:

After appraising the drawing, Richard informed Cynthia that her art was worthless.

To *apprise* is to give someone information:

In an urgent undertone, Donald apprised me of the worrisome situation.

Lose vs. Loose   To *lose* something is to misplace it or shake it off:

Michael tried to lose the hideous shirt his girlfriend had given him for Christmas.

Loose means movable, unfastened, or promiscuous:

The loose chair leg snapped off, and Doug fell to the floor.

Principal vs. Principle   The *principal* is the person who calls the shots in a school:

Principal Skinner rules Springfield Elementary School with an iron fist, yet he still lives with his mother.

A *principle* is a value or standard:

Edward, a boy of principle, refused to cheat on the test.

Eminent vs. Imminent   An *eminent* person is one who is well known and highly regarded:

The eminent author disguised himself with a beret and dark glasses.

An *imminent* event is one that is just about to happen:

When the paparazzi's arrival seemed imminent, the celebrities ducked out the back entrance.

Lie vs. Lay   To *lie* describes an action being performed by something or someone. To *lay* describes an action that needs to be done to something. The tricky thing to remember is that *lay* is also the past tense of the verb to *lie*:

Lie (lay, lain, lying)
Present tense: *I lie down on my towel and soak up the sun.*
Past tense: *I lay down on my towel and soaked up the sun.*

Lay (Lay, laid, laid, laying)

Present tense: *I lay the pencil on the desk and try to focus on the question.*

Past tense: *I laid the pencil on the desk and tried to focus on the question.*

Very Unique   *Unique* means "without like or equal." There are no degrees of uniqueness; if something is unique, it is one of a kind.

> Incorrect: *My cousin has a very unique personality.*
> Correct: *My cousin has a unique personality.*

Avoid Wordiness

You should do your best to be concise in your writing: use only the words you absolutely need. If you see phrases such as *being that* or *in regard to the fact that* or even just *the fact that* in your writing, you've fallen prey to wordiness. Here are red flags to look out for that suggest you need to make your writing more concise.

Unnecessary Definitions   Don't waste precious space explaining the obvious:

> *We rushed to the emergency room, a bleak place where people who are sick or who have been in an accident wait until a doctor can see them.*

There's no need to define "emergency room":

We rushed to the emergency room.

It is* and *There are   Avoid starting a sentence with *It is* or *There are*:

> Wordy: *It is my father who makes the decisions in my house.*
> Better: *My father makes the decisions in my house.*

> Wordy: *There are some people who just don't know when to stop writing.*
> Better: *Some people just don't know when to stop writing.*

Personally* and *I think   You can leave out *personally* and *I think* because the reader knows the words on the paper are your beliefs:

> Wordy: *I think the Patriot Act provides the government with abusive police powers and methods to invade our privacy.*
> Better: *The Patriot Act provides the government with abusive police powers and methods to invade our privacy.*

Two Words Rather Than One   Don't use two words to say the same thing:

> *I was happy and thrilled when my uncle told me he was visiting.*

Choose the stronger word and delete the other. Similarly, you may have two sentences that say pretty much the same thing, just in slightly different ways. It's tempting to use both, but decide which one is stronger and cut the other.

Be Parallel

In every sentence, all of the different components must start, continue, and end in the same, or parallel, way. It's especially common to find errors of parallelism in sentences that list actions or items. For example:

> *In the pool area, there is no spitting, no running, and don't toss your half-eaten candy bars in the water.*

The first two forbidden pool activities end in *–ing*, and because of that, the third forbidden must also end in *–ing*. Everything in your list must be the same:

> *In the pool area, there is no spitting, no running, and no tossing your half-eaten candy bars in the water.*

Punctuate Correctly

Using punctuation correctly is vital to ensuring your essay is effective. Punctuation sometimes comes naturally, but this doesn't mean it's always *correct*. You need to know the basic rules so you can proofread your work thoroughly.

Commas   When you join two complete sentences with conjunctions such as *and*, *but*, or *for*, place a comma before the conjunction:

> *I want to go, but it is snowing.*

If you're unsure whether you need a comma, check to see if the subject changes over the course of the sentence. If it does, you need a comma:

The parrot squawks obscenities, and the dog eats nothing but steak.

If there is no subject following the conjunction, you don't need a comma:

The parrot squawks obscenities and eats nothing but crackers.

Ultimate Style

Do not join independent clauses (complete sentences) with a comma. Instead, use a period or a semicolon:

Incorrect: *It is about to snow, we'd better not go.*
Correct: *It is about to snow; we'd better not go.*
Correct: *It is about to snow. We'd better not go.*

Be sure to enclose parenthetical statements in commas:

My father, an avid skier, wants to move to Colorado.

Use a comma to separate parts of a date or an address:

My niece was born in Morristown, New Jersey, on May 24, 2002.

Be sure to separate items in a list with commas. You can put a comma between the final two items or leave it out—both ways are correct:

> Correct: *Chocolate, pizza, pasta, and ice cream are my favorite foods.*
> Correct: *Chocolate, pizza, pasta and ice cream are my favorite foods.*

Colons and Semicolons   A semicolon indicates a pause between two complete sentences. It is stronger than a comma but weaker than a period:

> *My father has a wonderful sense of humor; nevertheless, he is a strict man.*

The colon means "as follows":

> *There are five stages of grief: denial, anger, bargaining, depression, and acceptance.*

It should not be used to introduce a short list:

> Incorrect: *I went to the store and picked up: corn on the cob, hamburger meat, and beefsteak tomatoes.*
> Correct: *I went to the store and picked up corn on the cob, hamburger meat, and beefsteak tomatoes.*

A colon can also be used to introduce a single word or phrase, to show a close connection between the two parts, or to add dramatic effect:

> *There was only one problem with her theory: she had no proof.*

Quotation Marks   Commas and periods always go inside the closing quotation mark:

> *"I ate too much," said my little brother.*
> *My little brother said, "I ate too much."*

The first word of a quotation is capitalized, but if you interrupt the quote don't capitalize the first word of the continuation:

> *"Because of your rude behavior," said Mr. Smith, "you can't come on the class field trip."*

Exclamation Points   Do not use exclamation points to strengthen weak words. The exclamation point should be used only for true exclamations or for commands (*Stop!*). You'll rarely use exclamation points in essays.

Check Your Spelling

Relying heavily on word-processing programs that check your spelling can get you into trouble by lulling you into a false sense of security. For example, they don't detect if you use the wrong word; they notice only if a word is spelled incorrectly. If you're not careful, you might miss the fact that you wrote the word *compete* when you meant to write *complete*.

A Final Note

Learning to write an excellent essay is an ongoing process. Every essay you write will be different—each will be written for a different class and with a different purpose, and each will address a different topic. Each time you sit down and begin brainstorming or writing a first draft, you'll have to start from the very beginning. However, understanding the basic essay-writing process will help take the mystery out of writing—no matter what kind of essay you're working on, you'll know exactly what to do, every step of the way.

Like anything else, practice makes perfect. As you write, you'll discover your own writing style and your own best strategies for finding a topic, creating a thesis, developing arguments, outlining, writing a rough draft, and revising. You'll work out the kinks and see how all the parts work together to help you write an excellent essay, every time.

Don't let that blank page or computer screen scare you off! Now you know what to do, so you can get started. Good luck!

Permission Credits

About the Author

Justin Marshall, a teacher, writer, and filmmaker, received a
B.A. from Macalester College and an M.F.A. from the Film
Program at Columbia University. He has taught English at a
junior high school in Japan and Film History and Directing at
Columbia University, and he has served as an Adjunct Professor
for the Digital Filmmaking program at the Katharine Gibbs
School in Manhattan. He lives in New York City.